The Mentor's Way

Drawing on the author's extensive experience in training mentors, *The Mentor's Way* outlines eight rules for engaging in a mentoring relationship. Nemanick examines the ways in which mentoring differs from managing or leading, and details the various roles of the mentor as a role model, motivator, confidant, coach, and more. Readers will learn how to develop successfully in each of these roles while helping a protégé to develop his or her own skills.

Clear and elegant chapters, each prefaced with a real-world example, emphasize to readers that their role as a mentor lies in listening and responding to a protégé's individual strengths and needs. Special attention is paid to creating a safe space, displaying empathy, and fielding a protégé's questions while knowing what to ask as a mentor. The author takes the anxiety out of the mentoring journey, accompanying practical insight with chapter exercises that are designed to help readers use their own experiences to identify best practice. Suggested topics for difficult mentor/protégé conversations allow readers to facilitate a stronger, more open relationship with their protégé.

This practical guide will provide mentors with the toolkit they need to get the most out of a relationship with their protégés.

Rik Nemanick, PhD, is a principal with The Leadership Effect, a leadership development consulting firm based in St. Louis, USA. He trains 750–1,000 mentors each year through formal mentoring programs in the corporate setting, and has worked with Monsanto Company, Build-A-Bear Workshop, and Massachusetts General Hospital, among other organizations.

Not only does Nemanick properly encourage us to broaden the traditional definition of a mentor—more importantly, he provides actionable advice about how to become a more impactful mentor within this expanded definition. By realizing that mentoring can range from a single inspiring interface to a formal relationship with a protégé, people in leadership positions should feel moved, if not obligated, to share their knowledge and experience more readily to bring out the best in others.

Sharon John, *CEO of Build-A-Bear Workshop, USA*

The Mentor's Way
Eight Rules For Bringing Out the Best in Others

Rik Nemanick

Routledge
Taylor & Francis Group
NEW YORK AND LONDON

First published 2017
by Routledge
711 Third Avenue, New York, NY 10017

and by Routledge
2 Park Square, Milton Park, Abingdon, Oxon OX14 4RN

Routledge is an imprint of the Taylor & Francis Group, an informa business

© 2017 Taylor & Francis

The right of Rik Nemanick to be identified as author of this work has been asserted by him in accordance with sections 77 and 78 of the Copyright, Designs and Patents Act 1988.

All rights reserved. No part of this book may be reprinted or reproduced or utilised in any form or by any electronic, mechanical, or other means, now known or hereafter invented, including photocopying and recording, or in any information storage or retrieval system, without permission in writing from the publishers.

Trademark notice: Product or corporate names may be trademarks or registered trademarks, and are used only for identification and explanation without intent to infringe.

Library of Congress Cataloging in Publication Data
A catalog record for this book has been requested

ISBN: 978-1-138-18990-4 (hbk)
ISBN: 978-1-138-18991-1 (pbk)
ISBN: 978-1-315-64136-2 (ebk)

Typeset in Sabon
by Out of House Publishing

To Coke Hennessy and Rich Nemanick
My Parents, and First Mentors

Contents

	Foreword	viii
	Acknowledgements	x
1	Overview	1
2	Lead by Following	15
3	Chart a Course	32
4	Create a Safe Place	50
5	Good Questions Beat Good Advice	63
6	Balance Empathy and Action	79
7	Foster Accountability	96
8	Fill the Toolkit	110
9	Honor the Journey	128
	Index	135

Foreword

High school graduation. Is there a scarier time in a young person's life? I challenge you to think of another time in your life where EVERYTHING changed. Marriage? Yes, there is change. But you are still you. Having a child? Again, a big deal. But hopefully you have a built-in support network that will guide you through it. But graduating from high school and headed off to college, a job, or the military? Forget about it. Everything changes.

Earlier this year, upon the occasion of one of my sons' high school graduation, I attended a slew of graduation parties. The first few were all the same ... the kids accepting congratulations and nervously answering questions about what lies ahead for them; moms talking about dorm room furniture; and dads standing back having a beer, wondering when it will be over so they can get on with their Saturday duties (or tee times). Then, out of the blue, I was approached by a now eighteen-year-old young man who I had coached in little league baseball from the ages of eight to fourteen, whom I hadn't seen in a few years. He said, "Mr. Mannis? Graduation has really got me thinking about how I became the person I am today. If you have a few minutes, I'd like to say thanks for all that you did for me." He went on to tell me stories about how he appreciated my style of coaching, how I inspired him to be his best, how I helped him see challenges as opportunities, and how he even looked to me in place of his own dad a few times, when he was really questioning his desire to continue with the sport.

I can honestly say I will never forget that moment. I never really realized it, but I made a profound impact on that young man's life. And, hopefully, you are already seeing the parallels between my story and the topic of this book—mentoring.

Other than being a retired little league coach, my "day job" for the last twenty-five years has been focused in Human Resources, which has to date culminated in the role of Senior Vice President of Human Resources for a \$1.3 billion global manufacturer that has just under 6,000 employees around the globe. In this role, I have a few priorities. The one I take the most seriously is this—*Ensure that we have our best people working on our most important things.* Sounds simple, right? However, as we have explored this philosophy, we have realized a few things, including the question, "what if one of our best people has never done *that* thing on which we want him or her to work?" As we were pondering the answer, we found that one path has worked the best: pair the "best person" with someone who has done that work before, to help speed his or her learning curve. Or, conversely, pair one of the "best people" with one (or a few) people who need help, to teach them the way.

It was at this point that I brought in Rik Nemanick—your guide (and author) of this book—to work with twenty mentors and twenty protégés who represented the future leadership of our company. I can honestly say that the steps detailed in *The Mentor's Way* have provided a real-life, digestible, and effective path for both groups to help take individual and organizational performance to the next level (which is the real goal, right?).

But I have also seen a deeper, almost more meaningful outcome from this work that relates back to my story of the young baseball player. I made an impact on him—deeper and larger than I imagined at the time. And, now that I look back on it, I can truly say that he made an impact on me, too. I have many examples from both mentors and protégés in the workplace that are exactly the same. Relationships that went on to take people to heights that they never imagined.

So, in closing, I congratulate you for picking up this book, and for beginning your journey down *The Mentor's Way* ... one that will be rewarding, fulfilling, and maybe even life-changing.

Scott Mannis, Ph.D.
Senior Vice President of Human Resources
Hussmann Corporation
Contributor to *The Real-Life MBA*, by Jack and Suzy Welch
St. Louis, MO

And just in case you're wondering, my team—The Falcons—did win our league championship ONE time in seven years. So, at least I have that.

Acknowledgements

Any book on mentoring should acknowledge the author's mentors. I have many mentors who helped me with different parts of my journey. Carol Weisman has been my writing mentor. Her support and guidance helped me find my writing voice for this book and helped me figure out how to fit writing a book in around raising a family and growing a consulting business. Margo Murray's book *Beyond the Myths and Magic of Mentoring* got me started in the field of mentoring when I was first discovering it. She also provided me with some great advice in writing the book along the way. Two of my clients, Jeff Veenhuizen at Monsanto and the late Kim Knight at Boeing, challenged me to develop my thinking about mentoring and improve the work I was doing for their respective companies. They pushed me to develop my skills as a consultant and as an expert in mentoring.

My business partner, Bob Grace, has shown great patience as I have grown as a consultant. His years of experience and supportive feedback have helped me mature in my field. Alan Weiss, whom I only met once at a talk he gave over a decade ago, inspired me in the early days of my consulting. His audaciously titled book, *Million Dollar Consulting*, gave me a blueprint that helped my business grow from a handful of clients to becoming a trusted advisor to dozens. And, Bob Vecchiotti was the solo consultant I met early on who got me to believe I could do it. He was a great source of optimism for my early consulting career. Whenever I would feel disheartened about my work, my wife would tell me to go meet with Bob to find my positivity again.

The two biggest inspirations for me before I became a consultant were professors at Saint Louis University. Jerry Katz was a psychologist who taught in the management department. He was a great source of ideas and encouragement. He helped me find my way as I was finishing my graduate degree, navigating the waters out of the comfort of academia into the business world. Dave Munz was my graduate school advisor who took a chance on me. He shepherded my early graduate career and taught me a lot about being a psychologist.

Acknowledgements xi

I tell the stories of the next two mentors in the pages of the book. Brother Eugene Feld, a Marianist brother at Chaminade College Preparatory, planted seeds of confidence and self-concept that are still growing today. And, Marvin McMillan was a confidant, guide, and inspiration who helped me find my way during my early twenties when I had no idea what I wanted my career to be about.

I dedicate this volume to my first two mentors, Rich Nemanick and Coke Hennessy. Aside from raising me to adulthood, they both served as role models for my professional life. My mother built a successful solo law practice in the 1970s when few women were doing so, making a name for herself and a reputation as a consummate professional. My father took an unconventional path for a lawyer by leading his family business, Lorvic, after the passing of my grandfather. He taught me many lessons about growing a business and being a father.

Finally, I would like to thank my beautiful wife, Dawn. Not only has she shown enormous patience as I pursued my career and took time to write this book, she has inspired me to be a better person. She always pushed me to have an open mind and to look for the good in people. She found the good in me eighteen years ago.

1 Overview

I sat across the desk from the vice president of human resources. His office could be an imposing place. The tinted windows filtered the light so that, even on a sunny day, it still appeared dimly lit. The desk between us was huge and impeccably uncluttered. Marvin leaned back in his large, leather executive's chair to ponder what I had just told him as he played with his tie. He was a large man in his fifties, and wore a very stylish, very dark three-piece suit. He stared so intently at a spot in mid-air somewhere over my shoulder I almost turned around to see what was there. After what seemed like an hour of silence, he took off his glasses and leaned forward again with a serious look on his face. He said, "That is a lot to digest, Rik. I could tell you what I would do in your situation, but I'm more interested in what you think you should do next."

The simple question that hung in the air between us was at once full of possibilities and weighed down by responsibility. It was empowering and frightening. I had come to my mentor seeking an answer to allay my fears. While he could have told me what to do and alleviated my doubts about making the wrong choice, he demonstrated his care and belief in me through a question. It took longer than simply giving me advice, but its impact was more profound and long-lasting.

That conversation was just one in a series of discussions I had with my mentor, Marvin McMillan. He was not my first mentor, nor will he be my last. But, it was my relationship with him that was part of the genesis of my love of mentoring and the foundation of this book. He saw something in me that I did not know was there, and took the time to bring it out of me. He was a role model, a sounding board, a thought provoker, and an accountability partner. He was my mentor when I was twenty-two and at a pivotal juncture in my career, shepherding me to a new chapter that started me on the path I still follow today.

Without knowing it, he also taught me a lot about mentoring itself. Like many veteran mentors, he made mentoring look easy and effortless. It is only in retrospect that I recognized what he was doing as a mentor and how it affected my growth, understanding, and confidence. Marvin

2 Overview

and the mentors who both preceded and followed him built the foundation for this book. This work is the cumulative wisdom of my own mentors, as well as the thousands of mentors in dozens of organizations whom I have taught, who at the same time taught me about one of the most gratifying roles you can play for someone else. Before going any further, it might help to define the basic word: mentor.

What is a Mentor?

A mentor is much more than a teacher or a guide. Being a mentor is a role which encompasses many faces of a relationship with a protégé. In its simplest form, a mentor is an experienced senior who is on a journey with a junior, helping the junior learn and grow along the way. The help a mentor provides will take many forms: The mentor can teach a protégé about an organization's culture. The mentor can advise a protégé about how to handle a particular situation. The mentor can inspire a protégé through words of encouragement. The mentor can revitalize a protégé to take the next step or after a setback. Mentors do all of these things and more as they experience the protégé's journey.

> A mentor is on a journey with a protégé.

It would help to pause for a moment to think about the mentors you have encountered on your journey so far. Who have they been? Why do you consider them mentors? What did they do? What did they mean to you? Did they open doors for you? Did they encourage you to go beyond self-imposed limits? Were they there when you were experiencing difficulty? Did they inspire you? Did they even know you thought of them as a mentor?

A quick exercise here might help with our definition. Write down the names of your mentors. You can define "mentor" as loosely as you wish since this is your list. You could include teachers or coaches in high school. You could name a professor in college, or a first boss. You might write the name of an important rabbi, pastor, imam, or other spiritual leader. Your list might even include a camp counselor or a parent. Their impact may be large or small. List at least ten mentors.

1.	6.
2.	7.
3.	8.
4.	9.
5.	10.

How easy was it to come up with ten? Were you able to get ten names out with relative ease? Or, did you struggle to come up with a handful? If you struggled, was there someone that caused you to hesitate? Did you say to yourself, *That person was important, but I don't know if I'd use the term "mentor"*? If so, go back and add the name to the list. Part of being a mentor for someone else is recognizing all of the people who have helped make you who you are today. They all can teach you lessons about mentoring without even recognizing at the time that they were a mentor to you.

For example, an early mentor of mine was Bro. Eugene Feld, my pre-Calculus and Calculus teacher in high school. Until my junior year, I was a relatively consistent B student in my math courses. About halfway through my junior year, Bro. Feld and I were reviewing one of my tests where I didn't quite live up to my B average. We were talking about a question that I should have gotten right, but I had rushed through and made an easy mistake. He stopped, put his pen down, looked at me and said, "C'mon, Rik. You're smarter than this." He saw talent within me that I hadn't fully developed, and his single sentence challenged me to live up to it. I'm certain that he never gave that interaction another thought; I was just one of sixty students he taught each year in a career that began before either of my parents were born. But, after that, I started to let my talent grow. I had all A's in Calculus in my senior year, achieving a 5 on the AP exam, a program Bro. Feld pioneered at the school and for which he was passionate. I spent three years in college tutoring students in statistics and economics, and I cut my teeth teaching statistics for five years in graduate school.

That one encounter—that one sentence—was a catalyst that helped change the way I think about myself. At the time, I do not think I recognized the impact his confidence had on my self-concept. In fact, I probably would not have thought of him as a mentor at the time. But, his impact on my journey was as significant as any other mentoring I have had. My only regret is that he died before I got the chance to thank him for his gift.

Bro. Feld and I did not have a long relationship like Marvin and I did, but he was a mentor nevertheless. He was there at an important moment and changed how I thought about myself. If you are having trouble completing your list, find the people whose roles seemed small but whose impact was large. Make sure you come up with at least ten names so you can start to recognize all of the mentors who had something to teach you.

Look over your list a few times. Take yourself back to the time on your journey when each of them was a mentor to you. Think about how each one changed your thinking, helped you figure out a path forward, celebrated a success, or picked you up when you stumbled. You may not have thought of some of them as mentors until just now, but you can see how each of them was there for part of your journey.

For the second part of the exercise, go back to the list of mentors and pick your top three. Your selection could be the mentors who were with you the longest, who had the biggest impact, or who helped you make a critical decision at an important inflection point. Write their names on another piece of paper or in the space below. Then, to the right of each name, write five words or phrases that define each individual as a mentor to you.

4 Overview

	Name	Descriptors
1.		
2.		
3.		

Did you write words like "teacher," "good listener," or "guide?" Maybe you wrote "advisor," "role model," or "saw something in me." As you read over your list, consider how different your mentors are. While they may have a few descriptors in common, each played a different role for you. As you can see, there is no one attribute or activity that encompasses the entire role of mentor. In fact, if we were to amend the earlier definition of mentoring, it might read "a mentor is an experienced senior who is on a journey with a junior, *playing different roles* to help the junior learn and grow along the way." With this in mind, let us examine the diversity of roles mentors play.

Roles of the Mentor

Role Model: The first role mentors occupy is one that some mentors do not know they are portraying. Many protégés are drawn to a mentor whom they respect and admire, who is seen as a leader by others. In this role, the mentor is setting an example that the protégé wants to follow as a model of success. Some look for someone who inspires them to better themselves. Others want someone whose style aligns with their own so they can see a picture of how to achieve their goals in a way that feels authentic. Some mentors see this aspect of their role as intimidating, as if they are on a pedestal. But, the role model is foundational to many successful mentoring partnerships as it means there is a level of respect the protégé has that allows the other roles to take shape.

Inspirer/Motivator: While being a role model feels somewhat passive (the protégé is observing the mentor), being a motivator is more active. Mentors have the power to build energy within a protégé and focus that energy into action. I have used many of my own mentors this way; when I am getting bogged down in something important or difficult, I often reach out to a mentor to help pick me up and start moving again. A mentor can be a powerful ally to clear logjams and help a protégé see what is possible. The mentor can also help cope with nagging doubts that inhibit action and drain energy.

Confidant: As you will see later in this book, trust is the oxygen of mentoring. The trust between a mentor and protégé enables the protégé to take risks and stretch himself. To get there, he needs to begin building trust with a mentor by seeing the mentor as a confidant with whom he feels safe sharing his thoughts and feelings. All of us carry around with us a mixture of aspirations and apprehensions. A mentor who is a confidant gives us time and space to explore these emotions and how they affect us. When a protégé is able to see his mentor as a confidant, he becomes open to a greater world of mentoring.

Coach/Counselor: Once you have developed a trusting relationship with a protégé, it is natural that she will seek your advice on current challenges she is facing. These coaching opportunities are usually more tactical than the larger mentoring role you will play. But, being able to help solve these short-term issues helps build your credibility as a mentor and the trust between the two of you.

Sounding Board: As a protégé grows in confidence and experience, your role as a mentor may shift from playing an active advice-giving role to more of a sounding board, letting a protégé talk through his issues and solutions, looking to you more for validation than input. It is here that a well-thought-out question that gets the protégé thinking is more valuable than any advice that you could give.

Connector: As your relationship with your protégé grows, you will inevitably move from situations where you feel comfortable giving guidance or advice to topics beyond your experience or expertise. Many mentors fear the question to which they do not have an answer, but the best mentors see the next part of their role emerge. They realize that their vast network of connections is more valuable than any guidance they could give. Far from being a failure, the ability to connect a protégé with a resource in the mentor's network that could help becomes an extension of the mentoring partnership.

Advocate: The mentor's network often becomes a platform the mentor can use to help the protégé get visibility within an organization. The relationship that a mentor develops with a protégé gives her the capability to help the organization recognize talent within its midst. This advocacy role can be a natural outgrowth of getting to know a protégé's strengths, weaknesses, and aspirations. When a mentor is in a position to promote talent internally, both the protégé and the organization benefit.

Defender: Many of us can be misunderstood in our own organizations. Bad first impressions can curtail a promising career when they are held by the wrong people. There are times when a protégé needs help repairing a reputation. A mentor, by her status within the organization, is often in a position to defend a protégé and help him wipe his slate clean.

As you can see from the list above, being a mentor is more than just a set of attributes or activities. It is an interwoven set of roles. This collection of roles are what make a mentor one of the most powerful resources to develop people. A mentor can play different roles based on what the protégé needs at the time. Furthermore, different mentors can play

6   *Overview*

different roles for the same protégé. For instance, you might have one mentor you look to as a role model and another to whom you turn for guidance or advice.

As you review the list you created earlier, you will notice that different mentors have different gifts that help them play the role or roles that they performed for you. You will probably notice that not every mentor is very skilled at every role. One of my mentors was very good at giving advice. If I brought him a challenge with which I was struggling, he could rattle off three or four good ideas that I would not have come up with on my own. However, this same mentor had a lot of difficulty pivoting to being a sounding board who could ask the insight-provoking question. It in no way diminished his importance to me as a mentor; otherwise, I would not have gone to him for his insights as often as I did. But, I came to realize what I would get when I visited him and I used that to choose which issues I would bring to him.

The same holds for your role as a mentor. It is unlikely that you will be all things a mentor can be to a protégé. You will, however, have a lot of opportunities to have a positive impact on others with the talents that you do have. And, following the rules in this book will help you add to your skills as a mentor so that you can have a greater impact for good on others.

Roles and Relationship

At this point, you might be asking yourself, "I have given people advice and introduced them to people in my network. Was I a mentor to them?" This is not an easy question to answer since mentoring is often in the eyes of the beholder. What gives the mentor's role its power is the relationship the mentor has with the protégé. The protégé needs to feel some connection to the mentor that forms the basis of trust between them. Being a protégé requires a fair amount of openness and vulnerability. The protégé needs to feel that the mentor cares about him and wants to help him on his journey.

Like any relationship, mentoring cannot be forced. In fact, the status of mentor is often awarded retroactively. If you re-examine your list of mentors you created earlier, you may be able to identify the point when the relationship started to become mentoring for you. For some, you may not have thought of the person as a mentor at the time, but only now in retrospect see the relationship you had as mentoring. What you will likely see is a person who cared about you and who believed in you without expecting anything in return. You will see something akin to altruism, where the mentor played her roles without expecting anything in return.

> The status of mentor is often awarded retroactively.

Overview 7

It is this genuineness that imbues the roles the mentor plays with their power. It is this final amendment that will complete our definition of a mentor: **a mentor is an experienced senior who is on a journey with a junior, playing different roles to help the junior learn and grow along the way, who genuinely cares about the junior and has a sincere desire to help.**

Facilitated vs. Spontaneous Mentoring

Before going much further into the topic of mentoring, it might help to consider the topic of "formal vs. informal" mentoring. As noted earlier, the concept of seniors training juniors has been with us for centuries. Some professions use a formal process (e.g., apprenticeship, residency for physicians, etc.) to train juniors in the skills of the profession. But, when it comes to the broader role of mentoring, many people consider "informal" mentoring to be superior, saying that you cannot force a mentoring partnership. I would agree that mentoring cannot be forced. But, after working with thousands of mentors and protégés in structured programs across dozens of companies, I do believe that it can be facilitated. In fact, I tend not to use the terms "formal" and "informal," preferring instead "facilitated" and "spontaneous."

Spontaneous mentoring partnerships form all of the time. Two individuals feel some connection where a senior has an inclination to help a junior, and the junior is similarly driven to allow him or herself to be helped. The connection may form quickly or it may take years to develop. At some point, the trust between the two grows to the point where the protégé is sharing more sensitive topics with the mentor for perspective and guidance. As the partnership continues, the protégé grows and learns from the experience. Then, at some point, the relationship changes where the period of active mentoring comes to a close (we will look into this phase closely in the last chapter) and the nature of the relationship changes. These four phases (initiation, trust building, growth and learning, and transitioning) rarely have obvious markers in spontaneous mentoring, but they are all there.

Facilitated mentoring goes through the same phases. There is an initiation where the mentor and protégé find themselves in their roles. If they commit to the process, they can start building the trust that leads to growth and learning. And, there tends to be a prescribed end date that marks the period of transition. While the initial spark that drew a mentor and protégé together in spontaneous mentoring may be hard to replicate in a more formalized process, there are several elements that a well-facilitated mentoring program can add to the natural process.

Making New Connections. In spontaneous mentoring, protégés typically look for mentors within their immediate world. That may be why so many mentoring partnerships emerge from supervisor-subordinate

8   *Overview*

relationships. A facilitated process typically pairs protégés with mentors they may not know at all. They typically cross boundaries within the organization and create connections that are not likely to have formed on their own.

Accelerate the Process. The period of initiation and trust building often takes months or years in a spontaneous mentoring partnership. A facilitated process can provide enough structure for the mentor and protégé to find their mutual connection and create the foundation of their partnership within weeks.

Instruction to Maximize Impact. Many protégés in spontaneous mentorships are not prepared for their role and do not get as much out of the partnership as they could. Likewise, many mentors are not skilled in the various roles they play and miss opportunities to help their protégés grow. A facilitated training process can instruct both parties in their roles and help them get more out of mentoring.

Support Along the Way. Many spontaneous mentoring partnerships fade before they have to due to misunderstandings or miscommunication between the mentor and protégé. A facilitated process can provide support to pairs whose relationships are faltering to see if they can be repaired.

We place a lot of value on the spontaneous spark that is the start of a mentoring relationship. After witnessing thousands of successful mentoring partnerships that were arranged by their companies, I wonder if we are overestimating the ability of two people to find enough commonality to spark a partnership with a little help. A mentoring program cannot create a spark between two people, but it can tell them where the matches are.

Managers and Mentoring

One question that comes to mind is, Can managers be mentors to their subordinates? As has been mentioned already, many mentoring partnerships have their origins in boss–subordinate relationships. There are many managers who set aside time for each of their subordinates to have mentoring conversations with their direct reports, discussing larger aspirations and aspirational career paths. These conversations lay the groundwork for a longer-term relationship to form and for mentoring to continue even after the subordinate has changed roles and bosses. With that said, the truth is that being the boss and the mentor at the same time is very challenging. The nature of the boss–subordinate relationship has many attributes that interfere with the potential contained in a mentor–protégé relationship. These attributes create limits to what the mentoring side of their partnership can accomplish.

First, there is an interdependency between the manager and subordinate that does not exist between the mentor and protégé. The manager needs her direct report to perform and deliver results, and the subordinate

Overview 9

needs his manager to provide resources, direction, and decisions. This interdependence is built around the immediate tasks for which both are responsible, meaning much of the dialogue between them is for mutual coordination. The manager directs, the subordinate performs, the manager gives feedback, etc. Because so much of their relationship is bound up in their current work, the types of conversations mentors and protégés have often take a back seat to current work.

The net result is mentoring conversations, if they happen at all, usually occur on an annual or semi-annual basis. And, the conversation will often get moved if current work is taking precedence. Because an independent mentor has little or no involvement in the protégé's current work, the work is much less likely to interfere with the mentoring conversations. In fact, the conversations will happen more frequently and be solely focused on the protégé's agenda for mentoring instead of a boss's priorities for work.

The second challenge has to do more with the protégé's comfort in holding the mentoring conversation with the boss. Even if a boss is very diligent about holding career conversations with each of her subordinates monthly, she will likely have subordinates who don't feel comfortable holding open, honest dialogue about their long-term ambitions with their boss. Many subordinates may be uncomfortable talking about their aspirational career paths if those paths take them away from their current role. These subordinates may censor their conversations in ways that they think will make their manager happy despite her reassurances that she really wants their honest thoughts.

For instance, in an early mentoring program, there was a protégé who was frustrated with his career path and had gone on job interviews with other companies. He did not feel comfortable discussing the situation with his boss, in part because he felt his boss held the job he needed to progress. Fortunately, he was able to discuss the situation with the mentor he had been assigned, and had an honest dialogue about his frustrations. The mentor was able to create a safe place for the discussion and get the protégé's thoughts out into the open, where he was able to recognize that he had narrowed the focus of his career path and was missing more opportunities that he could (and did) pursue within the company.

In fact, there may be many issues they are uncomfortable discussing with their manager. They may have fears or doubts about their skills or the work that they are doing, which they would not want a boss to know. There may also be ideas they have that they want to test out with a mentor before presenting to the manager so they can come across as capable in the eyes of the boss. Despite the boss's efforts to put the subordinate's mind at ease to have an open dialogue, many subordinates will still have difficulty being honest with a boss in the same way they would with a third-party mentor.

10   *Overview*

Finally, there are many times when the topic the protégé most needs to discuss with a mentor is his relationship with his boss. Mentors serve as pressure relief for boss–subordinate frustrations. They also can help a protégé understand his boss's positions with a third-party perspective. And, mentors can coach a protégé on how to change the conversation with the manager in a way that mends the partnership.

So, while as a boss you can and should be holding mentoring conversations with all of your direct reports, do not expect all of those discussions to reach the potential true mentoring can. In fact, one of the best things you can do for your subordinates is to open up the dialogue to better understand their aspirations, and then refer them to mentors within your organization who can help them see the big picture from a different perspective. And, you should offer yourself as a mentor to others' subordinates in return.

Rules for Mentoring

This book is organized as a series of rules on how to be a great mentor. They are built on observation and experience of what works and what doesn't in mentoring partnerships. There is a growing body of academic literature that demonstrates the benefits of mentoring, but there isn't much research on how to be an effective mentor.

Mentoring isn't a checklist. There is no step-by-step way to do it right. It requires judgment and dynamic adjustment to the needs of the protégé. In fact, it is the dynamic nature of mentoring partnerships that make them so powerful: the mentor adjusts to the needs of the protégé. However, having rules helps a mentor recognize the protégé's situation and have guidance on how to respond. The rules serve as foundational principles that help you be more effective. They are guides that will tell a mentor which way to go in a particular situation.

Many pursuits have rules that, when followed, increase the chances for success. Two examples come from two of my passions: baking and running. For instance, one rule you learn pretty quickly in the field of baking is "no improvising." While you can get creative and change proportions when *cooking* (I'm always tinkering with my ingredients in guacamole), *baking* is a chemical reaction that requires a precise balance of ingredients to turn out right. Improvising with ingredients, while fun, usually delivers poor results.

In distance running, one rule is to "run within your heart rate," which means running at a pace that doesn't push you to your maximum. Running too fast early in a race depletes your energy stores and will slow down your finish. In my first half marathon, I ran the first two miles at a pace on par with my 5k times. I was excited and soaking up the energy of the crowd of 7,000 people running with me (I usually run with one

Overview 11

other person). By mile 11 of 13, I had depleted my stores and had to walk about three-quarters of the last two miles. I needed to heed the rule to pace myself, not give in to my naïve instincts as a novice runner. Follow these and other rules, and you will be more likely to bake a great soufflé or finish a marathon.

The same holds true for mentoring. The rules will help a mentor avoid mistakes and vastly improve the mentoring interaction. For example, one of my basic rules for mentoring is that "a good question beats good advice." While trying to help a protégé solve a difficult challenge, the novice mentor might see what she thinks is a course of action that will fix the issue. It is very tempting for the mentor to give this advice, especially since she can see that her protégé is struggling with this issue and thinks it is the mentor's job to give advice and solve the problem. Giving in to this temptation, however, violates one of the rules, and will rob the protégé of valuable learning and reflection. The temptation is similar for the inexperienced marathoner who gets excited at the start of the race and runs too fast. The experienced marathoner knows the rule and runs at a pace that doesn't tax his heart rate (and energy stores) too early. The experienced mentor knows that advice is the end of a conversation while a question is the beginning of one.

The first time you read this book, you may find yourself thinking, "I must not be a very good mentor; I don't do any of these things." Most of my mentors have broken several if not all of the rules I cover here. That fact in no way diminished the roles they played for me. In fact, the rules are not meant to be laws that, when broken, lead to disaster. When I ran that first half marathon, I still finished the race. I just didn't finish as well as I could have had I heeded the rule. When you ignore one of the rules, you won't irreparably harm your protégé. But, you and your protégé will have a better experience if you follow them.

For Whom is This Book Written?

This book is written for anyone who is in the position to guide another's growth and who wants to have a greater impact. It is written for the manager with twenty-five years in the company who wants to pass along her wisdom. It is also for the newly minted partner in a law firm who wants to help a junior associate learn the ropes. It is for the professor starting graduate students on their professional careers. It is for the senior engineer who wants a junior engineer to realize there is more to a career than the next project. It is for anyone who has the desire to do for others what some mentor did for you.

12 *Overview*

It is meant to be used as a resource and a reference by both mentors in spontaneous partnerships as well as those in facilitated programs. Each chapter is written around one of the rules and contains ideas, resources, and tools to support the rule. It is meant for mentors to get ideas of how to improve their skills. For mentors in facilitated partnerships, it should serve as a supplement to program training.

This book is the compiled wisdom of over fifteen years of teaching thousands of mentors how to hone the craft of developing others. As you may find as a mentor, you learn a lot by teaching others. I have learned a lot teaching others to be mentors in addition to mentoring others myself. My goal in writing this book is to help mentors find the patience and skill to play the role of mentor on someone else's journey. Everyone has the chance to have an impact on someone else. My hope is that this book helps that person by helping you.

Where Do We Go from Here?

For the remainder of the book, I will cover one rule per chapter. Each rule is explored in depth, with examples of the rule in practice, illustration of why it is important, and description of how to apply it. Many of the rules have tools that go with them that help you with your mentoring partnership. Below is a preview of the eight rules:

1. Lead by Following

One mistake many mentors make is to take over for the protégé, driving both the overall mentoring process as well as the direction the protégé takes. Just as you can't lead a horse to water, good mentors know you can't force mentoring on someone. Even though some protégés would welcome someone taking over their development for them, in the long run they are better off being the drivers.

2. Chart a Course

The best mentors make an effort to understand the protégé's goals, helping to shape them and using them to guide their mentoring conversations. This chapter lays out the four phases of exploration and how to set goals that are motivating and aligned with the protégé's needs.

3. Create a Safe Place

Creating a trusting environment is the first job of a mentor. The amount of progress a protégé makes is driven by how much she or he can trust a mentor. Trust allows protégés to explore difficult issues and tap into personal undercurrents that are not explored with others.

Overview 13

4. *Good Questions Beat Good Advice*

Some mentors think their job is to dispense advice to their protégés, advice the protégé is all too happy to accept. However, if all a mentor is giving is advice, the only thing a protégé learns is to bring problems for the mentor to solve. The best mentors know that good questions teach a protégé to think, enabling the protégé to truly grow.

5. *Balance Empathy and Action*

If a mentor has built sufficient trust, a protégé will start bringing the more challenging issues, many of which have caused the protégé grief. Some mentors get caught wallowing with the protégé, overdoing the empathy but yielding nothing. Other mentors drive past the emotional component of issues and decrease the valuable trust they have built. Mentoring is about knowing how to connect with a protégé and honor their hopes and fears while still moving a protégé toward some tangible action that will address the issue.

6. *Foster Accountability*

One of the most powerful things a mentor can ask a protégé is, "Remember what you said you were going to do between our last meeting and now? How did that go?" While mentoring conversations can be engaging, real growth happens when a protégé applies what is discussed. The subtle yet powerful accountability that a mentor creates can spur a protégé to action.

7. *Fill the Toolkit*

No mentor is going to have all the answers. There will come a time when a protégé presents an issue that the mentor doesn't know how to unravel. Rather than be intimidated by these issues, the best mentors help the protégé find resources that they can use. They connect the protégé to people in their networks and incorporate their learning into the mentoring process.

8. *Honor Transitions*

There is a natural life cycle to mentoring. Most active mentoring relationships reach a point where the need for mentoring diminishes. If the mentor has done a good job, the protégé will have reached a new plateau of development where he is ready to progress down the path without the mentor. Good mentors recognize this point as the outcome of a successful relationship. They use it as a time of reflection, celebration, and transition.

Conclusion

Every mentor I had gave freely of him or herself, sharing wisdom, experience, and guidance. Mentoring is a wonderful gift that should be shared; my goal is to help others find ways to share their experience with others and make a difference in others' lives. This book is intended to create a framework for anyone who wants to help another achieve her or his unique potential. It is for the mentor who genuinely cares about another person and has a sincere desire to play a role on a protégé's journey. Explore the rules contained in this book and find tools that will help you bring out the best in a protégé.

2   Lead by Following

Claudia stepped back from the whiteboard in her office, folded her arms as she read her work, and smiled. The pro/con list she had created evaluating three different career opportunities for her protégé, Alex, was comprehensive and painted a very clear picture of where he should focus his efforts for his career. She nodded vigorously as her smile grew.

Claudia had been asked to participate in her company's mentoring program and was assigned Alex, a bright young engineer who showed a lot of promise. When she read over his curriculum vitae before their first meeting, she saw a lot of potential in him. Their first few meetings went very well, with Claudia throwing out a lot of ideas that Alex wrote down, each time saying, "That's a great idea. I hadn't thought of that." He thanked her at the end of the meetings for taking the time and for giving him a lot to work on between their meetings.

At the start of this meeting, Alex asked if they could spend some time talking about career options for him. Claudia's face immediately lit up and she replied, "I've been waiting for you to ask that! I have some ideas that I wanted to share." She grabbed the tablet off her desk and started reading the options that she had worked up the day before. She got excited and talked quickly as she took Alex through the options and wrote her ideas on the whiteboard. As she surveyed her work on the board, she said, "I think it's fairly clear what path you should pursue!"

Claudia's smile faded quickly when she turned around and saw that Alex was not listening. Instead, he was looking at his phone and chuckling at what he saw there. Her excitement quickly yielded to anger as her mind raced. What is he doing? *she thought.* I have put in all of this work and he isn't even paying attention! *Alex looked up and saw the scowl forming on Claudia's face. His eyes widened as he braced himself for what was coming next.*

That was when Claudia realized what was happening. Her anger quickly gave way to embarrassment. "I've done it again, haven't I?" she asked out loud. Alex's wide eyes turned to puzzlement as he listened to her. She continued, "I took over and treated you like another problem to solve. I am sorry; I do that to my direct reports all the time, and I know

16 *Lead by Following*

*it frustrates them. Let's start over. What are **your** thoughts about career options?"*

Alex was fortunate to have a mentor who possessed the self-awareness to recognize when she was taking over and losing sight of the primary goal for mentoring: helping her protégé learn how to grow. She took over the process and started solving the problem her protégé presented, forgetting that solving one particular problem is less important that helping the protégé learn how to solve the problem. By losing sight of this goal, Claudia found herself breaking the first rule of mentoring: Lead by Following.

Her temptation to take over for her protégé is a familiar impulse for most mentors. It is natural for her to want to help Alex, and solving his problem seemed like a great way to help him. In fact, it is a natural way for mentoring to begin: a junior comes to a senior to get advice and guidance on how to solve an issue. The protégé looks to the mentor as someone who can lead him to the answers. Many naturally forming partnerships begin with a boss who can help a subordinate solve challenges, creating the foundation of a helping relationship. The mentoring partnership is then built on a dynamic where the mentor is the leader and the protégé is the follower.

This foundation, however, can give way to a relationship where the mentor ends up driving the partnership and the protégé becomes a passenger. When this happens, mentoring begins to break down: the protégé begins to lose ownership over his situation as the mentor takes over more. Resentment can build on both sides. The protégé can start to resent the mentor who takes over and treats the protégé like a problem instead of a person. The mentor, in turn, can resent the protégé for giving up and letting the mentor do all the work. In this chapter, we will explore the roots of this relationship dynamic, examine the signs of when it is occurring, and provide guidelines to keep it from happening.

Leading Comes Naturally

There are many forces that cause mentors to take the lead in their mentoring partnerships. Some of them are about the roles the mentor and protégé play. Some are about protégés yielding control. Some are about the mentors themselves and unlearning the habits that made them successful in their own careers. Below are some of the reasons mentors find themselves in the driver's seat with their protégés.

Role of mentor. The definition of mentoring, an experienced senior helping a junior, contains the seeds of the mentor leading. We typically let those with more experience and tenure lead us. It stems from other senior-to-junior relationships we have had in our lives: teacher-to-student, boss-to-subordinate, parent-to-child. The senior in most cases is expected to lead the junior by setting direction, making decisions, and creating accountability. When a mentoring relationship grows out of a boss–subordinate one, the first hurdle that often needs to be overcome is the redefinition of the roles.

Power differences. In addition to the senior-to-junior dynamic of the roles, there is usually a power imbalance between mentor and protégé. The mentor occupies a position with more authority and, in the eyes of many protégés, more importance. As a result, the protégé may be more likely to defer to a mentor's ideas and judgment because of the power difference. In addition, there may be some intimidation on the part of the protégé who is hesitant to question a mentor's guidance or even ask for a mentor's time because of this power difference.

Protégé wants a solution. Protégés often step back and let the mentor lead when they are solving problems together. The protégé has likely thought about the issue and has not come up with a solution yet, so she is seeking the mentor's input and guidance. Since she hasn't come up with an answer on her own yet, she may be very willing to let the mentor take over and solve it.

Protégé wants to transfer risk. Much more subtle than the desire for an answer is the desire to transfer risk for the solution to someone else. It may be so subtle that the protégé doesn't know that he is doing it. The protégé is attempting to step away from owning the solution and the repercussions if it fails. This impulse can arise when a protégé has made several attempts to solve the problem and they haven't achieved the desired outcomes yet.

Protégé not invested. There are times when protégés are actually not invested in mentoring itself and are "going along" with a mentor. This situation arises in natural partnerships when the mentor has a stronger desire to help the protégé than the protégé's desire for help. The mentor reaches out and sets up meetings with the protégé, who is not really interested in mentoring, but it is easier to go along with what the mentor wants than to tell the mentor she is not interested. It also manifests itself in facilitated mentoring when a protégé signs up for a program but loses interest in mentoring during the course of the program. It may be that he didn't understand the purpose of the program or the nature of a mentoring partnership. Or, he may have been invested early in the process but has lost focus on mentoring and is no longer invested in driving the process.

Mentor sees potential in the protégé. Often the mentor recognizes potential in a protégé who hasn't realized it yet. A protégé shows a lot of promise and the mentor wants to help draw that talent out and grow it, both to benefit the organization and to benefit the protégé. The mentor wants to step in and shepherd the protégé to realize her potential even if she hasn't shown the interest or desire in doing so.

18 *Lead by Following*

Mentor had a mentor who drove. Some mentors follow the model of the mentor who guided them. They see an example of a mentor who plays a very active role in driving the partnership and they are imitating that behavior. As mentioned in the opening chapter, many of my own mentors did not follow the rules in this book. It was only after working with mentors and protégés that I started to see other ways to be a mentor.

Mentor likes solving problems. Most mentors who have achieved personal and professional success are good at solving problems. They have achieved their status because they are good at figuring out a course of action and getting results. When a protégé presents a problem to solve, all of the mentor's instincts kick in and she starts to actively take on the problem. The point at which the shift happens is easily missed, especially if both the mentor and protégé are engaged in the topic and the conversation. It occurs when the mentor can see the solution (more precisely, *a* solution), but the protégé hasn't grasped it yet. It is at this point when many mentors begin to take over and start steering the protégé to the solution.

Mentor wants partnership to be successful. The last reason mentors give in to the temptation to lead is that they want both the protégé and the relationship to be successful. This feeling may come from concern for the protégé (I don't want to give up on him). It also can stem from the mentor's personal ego (I don't want to be seen as having a failed partnership). Or, it can come from a desire to help the organization (I don't want the company to lose his talent). In any event, the mentor may be trying to preserve a relationship that would be better to let go of or at least put on hold.

What Happens if the Mentor Leads?

At this point, you might agree with all of the points above but be asking yourself, *So what? Is it really bad for a mentor to drive a partnership? If a protégé wants me to take charge, shouldn't I? What is the harm?*

The harm comes when the mentor goes from being a resource to help the protégé on his journey to becoming the driving force for the journey. The harm comes when the protégé takes his foot off the gas, hands off the wheel, and becomes a passenger. When this happens, the protégé becomes less invested in his growth and less capable of driving his own learning. The prior section shows how many factors can push a mentor into the driving role. But, stepping in and taking the lead with the protégé begins to erode the protégé's ability to learn.

It helps to recognize that there are at least two fundamental ingredients that lead to meaningful growth. The first is **doing the work**. By that, I mean putting in the time and effort to grow. Think about the periods of your own journey where you felt like you grew the most. It may have been when you first entered a field where it felt like everyone around you knew more than you. Or, it could have been a time when you were going down a path that ultimately was not right for you. Maybe it was a time of personal trial and challenge when it was difficult to keep going, but it left you stronger in the end. What made the growth lasting and valuable was the work you did to go through it. Having a mentor there to help with advice, guidance, or a push in the right direction may have helped you, but it was you who did the work.

At the beginning of the chapter, Claudia stopped herself in part because she found herself doing the work for Alex. While he may have been appreciative of her effort, she was robbing him of the opportunity to learn. More importantly, she took away the chance to learn how to learn for himself. The goal of the mentor often is not to solve the problem in front of the protégé, but to help the protégé go through the process of learning so he learns how to solve the problem himself. All that Alex was learning with Claudia is to come to her when he needs the answers, which will ultimately stunt his growth.

> **The goal of the mentor is not to solve the problem, but to help the protégé learn how to solve the problem.**

Doing the work often means going through the struggle. By "the struggle," I mean spending time trying out solutions that do not pay off or work out. We often use the word "failure" to describe those attempts, but I prefer the term "struggle." Failure carries with it some finality, whereas struggle implies that you are still working your way to the solution.

Of course, as a mentor, it is hard to watch a protégé in the struggle. You do not like seeing the frustration on the protégé's face, especially when you can see the answer. Again, go back to times when you were in a struggle with an important issue. It was the five or ten things you tried that didn't work that made the thing that did work stick with you. Going through those setbacks and disappointments, and then persevering to try again, is what made the learning powerful. Claudia recognized that figuring out a career path was a struggle Alex needed to take on himself. She could support him with advice and guidance, but he was the one who needed to go through the struggle to find a course that he truly owned. In the end, you and your protégé need to, as venture capitalist Ben Horowitz said, "Embrace the struggle" (Horowitz, 2014, p. 250).

The other basic ingredient in growth is the motivation to grow. The motivation is complex and has many elements wrapped up in it. It is the ambition to become better than you are today. It is the energy to set the direction for your destiny. It is the drive to feel forward progress toward something meaningful. These various sources of motivation create within a protégé a "felt need" that drives her to do the work. It is what helps her struggle through the setbacks and persevere. It is what causes her to follow up and follow through on things she and her mentor discuss. It is

20 *Lead by Following*

what will cause her to keep a meeting with her mentor on the calendar rather than cancel it to get one more thing done on her to do list.

The problem for mentors with the felt need is that it exists solely within the protégé. There is nothing a mentor can (or should) do to create the felt need. Any need a mentor tries to create will never truly be felt by the protégé. This point can be hard for some mentors to accept, especially when they see the potential locked within the protégé. They can see what the protégé can become if she only worked at it. Until the protégé feels the need, however, she won't be able to elevate it over other priorities that place demands on her time. Nothing is more frustrating for a mentor than chasing a disengaged protégé who cannot identify her felt need. For it is the felt need that the mentor will follow.

All a mentor can do is try to help find the protégé's felt need and feed it. Think of it as a pilot light, a small flame that doesn't go out that ignites the furnace when energy is needed. The need can be starved of oxygen, being smothered by all of the other demands on the protégé. By creating time and space, you can help the protégé connect with the felt need and draw energy from it. By showing interest in the protégé and her journey, you can validate that it is okay for her to pursue the felt need and give her permission to make it a priority.

In the end, you can neither do the work nor create the felt need for the protégé. But, if you can lead by following, you can enable the protégé to achieve things she didn't know she could, and realize the potential that you, as the mentor, could see all along.

Set the Tone for the Partnership

As you embark upon a new partnership with a protégé, keep the ultimate goal of mentoring in mind: to help the protégé learn how to grow. In order to achieve that goal, the protégé needs to be in the driver's seat and take the lead for the partnership. This step is accomplished by actively empowering the protégé to lead. You want to set a tone for the partnership where the protégé feels comfortable asking for your time and reaching out to you. Some protégés have no problem doing this and are very willing to take the lead if given permission (some will even do so without explicit permission). There is, however, a spectrum of protégés who will hesitate to take the lead with you, instead deferring to your guidance and being tentative with their requests. They are the protégés who need the mentor to be explicit with the permission to lead, and may require some encouragement on your part to do so. There are many things you can do to set the tone at the beginning to empower your protégé.

Begin by making yourself available to your protégé. When I am asked what qualities define a good mentor, I always begin with a mentor who is available. When a client was launching a mentoring program a few years ago, the group vice president who was sponsoring the program also insisted that he be added to the mentoring pool. I told him that he probably should not participate because his schedule likely would not permit him to spend time with his protégés. He was adamant, and suggested that he have three protégés even though all of the other mentors in the program were only assigned one. Predictably, his HR director, who was administering the program, let me know that, three months in, he was reassigning the three protégés to other mentors since none of them was able to get onto his calendar.

Being available means giving the protégé explicit **permission** to ask for time on your calendar or reach out when he needs to talk. Being direct with the permission will signal the fact that you want to make the time available and that the protégé should feel comfortable asking for it. You may want to think about how much time you can reasonably make available to the protégé and give him an idea about how often he can ask to meet. Doing so gives the protégé an order of magnitude of how much time he can request. It lets the protégé who just saw you last week know if he can contact you today if something has come up. It also lets the protégé who wants to see you every day know whether you are available that frequently. A mentor once told me about a protégé who was contacting her at night and weekends early in the partnership. She needed to let him know the outer limits of her availability.

You may also need to consider how you like time being booked on your **calendar**. This point may seem relatively minor, but it has held up many protégés before. There was a protégé in a mentoring program who let three months go by without a meeting. I asked him why had so much time passed between meetings, and he replied that he had left a voicemail message for his mentor and had not heard back. He did not want to pester the mentor, so he said he was waiting for the mentor to get back to him. When I discussed it with the mentor, he recalled the message, saying, "I remember being on the road and calling into my work phone to check messages at 11:00 p.m. I remember writing down the message in my hotel room, but I forgot about it the next day. Why didn't he just book it in the calendar system?" When I asked the mentor whether he told him how he liked meetings booked, he said he probably hadn't told his protégé how he preferred to have his schedule managed. While the mentor might have blamed the protégé for not calling again, he realized that the protégé was probably hesitant to bother him and did not know the best way to get onto the mentor's calendar. While it is a small point, telling your protégé how to get onto your calendar lowers another barrier that prevents mentoring from forming.

These first two steps toward empowering a protégé to take the lead are part of **breaking down the power distance** that often exists between a mentor and protégé. Because mentors tend to be longer tenured and higher ranking in organizations than protégés, there tends to exist some

22   *Lead by Following*

distance between the two that manifests itself in beliefs the protégé holds about how important the mentor is and how she or he should be treated. Mentors are afforded respect and deference by many protégés because of their position in the organization. For many protégés, this perception is necessary for them to respect a mentor. Those protégés want someone who is seen as important in the organization or profession. The same perception, however, can cause the protégé to be more deferential to a mentor, maintaining a distance between the partners that will ultimately stunt the partnership and what it can achieve.

Begin breaking down the power distance by getting to know your protégé and letting her get to know you. You will find that a productive mentoring partnership is built on trust between mentor and protégé. This trust starts early in the process as the partners get to know each other, find what they have in common, and start to feel a connection. Devoting time early on to get to know each other will lay this foundation of familiarity and make the protégé feel like she can ask for your time. Even if you have worked with the protégé for a while and feel like you know her fairly well, you may be surprised by what you learn by devoting time to a good "get to know you" conversation.

Once you start to feel like a mentoring partnership is getting off the ground, devote a meeting to getting to know each other. To get the most out of it, hold this meeting over a meal. Over the years, I have gotten feedback from mentors and protégés alike that sharing a meal together helped accelerate trust no matter where they were in the formation of the partnership. Set aside work and ask each other a lot of questions to dig deeply into who each of you are and what formed your thoughts and motives. You should exchange résumés or curricula vitae before this meeting and ask questions to explore your professional backgrounds. The meeting should not feel like an interrogation. It should feel like two people sharing where their journeys have taken them to date, learning about the important thoughts, experiences, and drives of each partner. (See Chapter 4 for more ideas on how to hold this meeting.)

Part of breaking down power distance during this meeting is to share the **unedited version of your journey**. This meeting is not a job interview where you want to present your best face. Tell the stories of your failures just as well as your successes. Telling your protégé when you have failed makes you seem more human and accessible as well as letting her know that even successful journeys have had setbacks. In talking about your past, share the disappointments and mistakes that frustrated you. Being vulnerable with a protégé will help her feel more comfortable with you and build a bond more quickly.

Your unedited journey should also reveal the **crooked path of your career**. When we tell our stories, we tend to smooth out all of our detours and setbacks, making our career path appear as if everything happened in a linear fashion and by design. In reality, our journeys are anything

Lead by Following   23

but straight paths from childhood to today. Did you change majors more than once in college? Did you get the job you wanted when you entered the workforce? Did you realize that the career you thought you wanted at eighteen wasn't the one you wanted at twenty-eight or even thirty-eight? Did you run into a brick wall with your career aspirations and change direction? Did your company ask you to make a change that sent you in an entirely new and different direction? Did you put your career path on hold so a spouse could pursue hers or his? All of these turns on your journey reveal a path that is shaped by reality. Sharing the crooked path lets the protégé feel more comfortable with the changes of direction in her own journey as well as be comfortable with you.

In addition to getting to know the professional side of your protégé, take time to get to know his personal side as well. Building the partnership involves getting to know the whole person. Many times, when you do not find commonality in your professional side, you can find it on the personal side. There may be a hobby or interest you have in common. You can use questions like the ones below to explore the personal side as well:

1. When you have leisure time, what do you like to do?
2. What is your favorite food? Place? Sport? Outdoor activity? Indoor activity?
3. Do you have a significant other? Kids? Pets?
4. What trip have you taken that you enjoyed the most? What trip would you like to take that you haven't yet?
5. Whom do you admire personally?

Make a note of what you learn during this conversation, especially of things that are important to your protégé and his identity. You will start to see a fuller picture emerge of who your protégé really is. You will gain an appreciation for the complexity of his personality and the mix of values that shape how he thinks of himself and how he approaches life. A protégé of mine spent a number of meetings discussing different scenarios for a new trajectory for his career. Many of the scenarios would require a significant change to not only his lifestyle but that of his wife and young children. While our conversation focused on the options he wanted to explore, we were able to add a wider perspective, which included his wife and her career as well as the needs of his children, that created a more robust and meaningful conversation.

Get the Meetings Started

As you get to know each other and give your protégé permission to ask for your time, begin setting some **regularity to your meetings.** You will find that if you establish a rhythm to your schedule, you and your

24 *Lead by Following*

protégé will begin to build momentum in your partnership. If you are in a facilitated program, I recommend a somewhat accelerated schedule at the beginning. Try meeting **every other week** at first. Ask your protégé to schedule these meetings on your calendar so that he starts to drive the schedule. By establishing a rhythm to your schedule, your protégé will start to get comfortable owning the schedule and start to incorporate the mentoring meetings into his routine.

If you are not in a facilitated program but rather see a mentoring relationship forming more naturally, you can still suggest regular meetings with your protégé. While there is no hurry to get into mentoring (you don't have the clock ticking down on a year-long relationship like those in formal programs), you do want to set a rhythm to your meetings that lets your protégé know that you would like to meet on a somewhat regular basis and that he should feel comfortable booking time. If every other week feels too aggressive for your partnership, consider something between **every three weeks** and **every six weeks**, with once a month being a reasonable middle point. Letting more time pass between meetings is not necessarily a bad thing and may fit with your protégé's needs. Some protégés are only looking for advice from time to time and are not interested in a more powerful partnership. But, many protégés would like more contact and will hesitate to ask for it if they don't feel like you are available. Setting an expectation that you would like to meet regularly empowers the protégé to ask for your time and get on the calendar.

In addition to talking about the frequency of your meetings, mentors in both facilitated and natural partnerships may also want to consider the **duration of meetings**. The default setting on many scheduling programs is typically an hour, so we have grown accustomed to having all of our meetings be an hour long. Rather than just going with the default, consider varying the length of your mentoring discussions. For your "get to know you" meeting, you may want to set aside ninety minutes or more over lunch to take the pressure off of the discussion. You want a relaxed discussion where neither of you is watching the clock and thinking about the work that is waiting for you back at the office. You may also try out more frequent thirty-minute meetings. The shorter duration is less likely to get canceled and may focus the conversation more. Many mentoring pairs strike a balance by meeting for one hour once a month and for thirty minutes between the hour-long meetings. This pattern keeps a more frequent meeting cycle without the protégé feeling like he has to have sixty minutes' worth of topics to discuss every time. There is no magic formula that works for every partnership. You should experiment with different combinations of frequency and duration to find out what will work for you and your protégé.

Another consideration is the **location** where you will meet. An obvious location to meet is your office. You always have access to it (unlike conference rooms, which seem to always be booked) and you are comfortable there. Most of my meetings with Marvin McMillan (my mentor in the first chapter) were in his office. While that location was very convenient for my mentor, it was also an imposing, intimidating place. Your office looks different to your protégé than it does to you, and can inadvertently reinforce the power distance between the two of you. Also, your subordinates know where you are and may not hesitate to interrupt your mentoring conversation. Instead of your office, find other places to meet, including your protégé's office, those overbooked conference rooms, or establishments like coffee shops outside the office. Find relaxed settings that will minimize distractions. One of my own protégés preferred to meet over lunch about twenty minutes away from her office to reduce the chance we would be interrupted by one of her coworkers, whom she frequently encountered at restaurants near her work.

Also consider the **communication media** options you have available to you. What is the easiest, most reliable way for your protégé to get hold of you? Let her know what it is and let her know that she can use it. Just like you want your protégé to feel comfortable scheduling time on your calendar, you should also let her know how to request an ad hoc meeting, especially if you don't work in the same office. There was a protégé located in Argentina who was working with a mentor in the US in a facilitated mentoring program. Both of them logged onto the company's instant messaging system every day (something the mentor had not done before) so that the protégé could see if his mentor was online and available for a quick discussion. He was able to reach out to her just as easily as someone who worked down the hall from her even though he was an entire hemisphere away. Finally, remember that you can also hold mentoring conversations over the phone. Sometimes, when your calendar has been taken over by a busy travel schedule, a lot of time can slip by between in-person meetings. Rather than lose momentum working together, schedule a thirty-minute phone call to keep in contact while you are on the road.

Mentoring at a Distance

Many mentors wonder about that last point about holding mentoring conversations over the phone. Can effective mentoring be done at a distance primarily over the phone? A partnership in an early mentoring program I facilitated provides a good example. Maria and Patty were enrolled in their company's mentoring program and were both enjoying the experience. They hit it off right away and set a good cadence to their meetings. Both of them looked forward to their meetings and regularly talked about how much they were getting out of the experience. After about five months, Maria, the protégé, accepted an opportunity to move to the company's plant outside of London, thousands of miles from the company's headquarters in Saint Louis. Her next meeting with Patty was

26   *Lead by Following*

going to be bittersweet. While the opportunity in the UK was just the type of career move they had been talking about, she was sorry that they were going to have to end their mentoring partnership early.

"That's ridiculous," Patty said. "I'm pretty sure that they have phones and the Internet in London. I don't want to end our mentoring just when you were achieving some of your goals. We will figure this out." They spent the rest of that meeting talking about how they could keep mentoring going across a long distance. They agreed to increase their meeting schedule from monthly to bi-weekly. They also looked at the time zone difference and decided that they would have their calls at 6:00 a.m. US Central Time, which was noon in London. Patty's willingness to work with Maria at a distance strengthened their partnership and helped Maria navigate the complexities of her new challenge.

Little solid empirical research has been published directly comparing in-person mentoring and mentoring conducted at a distance. Several of my clients have blended programs, where some of the participants met in person and others met over the phone. When we have surveyed the two groups, we have found no significant differences in their reported satisfaction with the program, with the progress they make together, or with their interpersonal relationship. While meeting in person is always desirable, geography does not have to be a barrier to mentoring. In fact, I have observed that mentoring partners are often even more intentional about their mentoring and create a more supportive structure than partners who meet in person. Below are some tips to follow when working with a protégé at a distance (several of these tips are good for in-person mentoring as well):

- **Set a recurring schedule**. Find a day of the week and a time of the day that will work for the both of you and set a recurring meeting on your calendars. The meetings during the first few months may be difficult, as they may come into conflict with other commitments, but you will find that you start to schedule your meetings around the mentoring calls going forward.
- **Set a more aggressive schedule**. When a meeting gets canceled, it can be hard to get one back on your calendar. If you had to cancel a meeting on your calendar tomorrow with someone, how far into the future would the two of you be able to reschedule? Scheduling more frequent meetings means that, when one gets canceled, there is likely one close behind it that is already on the calendar. In fact, if you have a schedule like that, you can give your protégé permission to cancel a meeting if there is not an important update since you know there is one just around the corner.
- **Schedule during "quiet" times**. If you are a few time zones away from each other, you may have a smaller window in which to book your calls. Consider scheduling calls during the beginning or the end

of your work day. Those calls are less likely to get interrupted or be rescheduled for other meetings. While the 6:00 a.m. schedule Patty set with Maria may be earlier than you would want to commit, you may find a 7:00 or 7:30 a.m. meeting is easier for you to keep on your calendar.

- **Be flexible with time zones.** Many of my clients have global programs where the protégé and mentor have hour-long windows where their schedules overlap. Naturally, one of you will be inconvenienced. Be flexible with this schedule and trade off who is inconvenienced. Many protégés will naturally defer to you and your schedule. Offer to schedule some of the calls during your protégé's normal working hours.
- **Use multiple media.** While many of your mentoring calls may be voice-only calls, don't overlook the impact of a video call, which will bring back a lot of the nonverbal cues and eye contact that gets lost over the phone. You can have your protégé practice a presentation as well so you can give feedback on her style.
- **Keep notes during your calls.** The opportunity to take good notes on your computer is actually an advantage for those meeting at a distance. When meeting in person, taking notes during a discussion can be somewhat awkward. You usually break eye contact to write down your thoughts, and the protégé may get self-conscious if you are writing down what she says. When you are meeting over the phone, you can take detailed notes, which may be easier to read than your own handwriting. I regularly find myself referring to meeting notes during my mentoring calls to provide context for the discussion.
- **Give virtual tours.** Participants in some of our global programs have put together slide shows for their partner about their workplace and themselves. They include photographs of their office, plant, or lab, of their coworkers, and even of their families. Others have used a video call to walk through their workplaces to give live, guided tours. Such tours help you and your protégé get better connected and give life to some of the topics you will be discussing.
- **Hone your listening skills.** Meeting at a distance will give you an opportunity to develop your own listening skills. Even video calls can have audio that is more difficult to hear than if your protégé were sitting across from you. You should eliminate other distractions so you can focus on what your protégé is saying.
- **Be mindful of language differences.** Many global mentoring pairs come from different cultures and different languages. Some mentors fail to recognize this fact and speak in their native language at a speed to which they are accustomed with other native speakers. Slow down if you normally speak quickly, and ask for feedback on how well your protégé understands you. Also, don't be afraid to ask your protégé to repeat himself if you are having a hard time understanding.

28　*Lead by Following*

- **Compare travel schedules.** Several years ago in a global mentoring program, the protégé in one of the pairs was attending a conference. He was on the last day of the conference, attending the last session before he left for the airport. When he looked at the speakers for the session, he was surprised to see his mentor's name listed as a discussant. While at first he found it a humorous coincidence that his mentor was speaking at the conference he was attending, he quickly realized that, had he known they were at the same conference together, they could have spent time meeting in person. In fact, in this particular program, mentors and protégés rarely had the chance to meet in person. I recommend you and your protégé compare travel schedules every few months to see if serendipity will work in your favor.

General Partnership Maintenance

All mentoring pairs should reflect on their meeting patterns and discuss whether they want to make any changes. About every three months, talk about how often you have been meeting and see if it is meeting both of your needs. Decide whether you want to accelerate the schedule or cut back if you are going into a busy time of year. Discuss whether you want to make changes to frequency, duration, or venue.

In addition to a general discussion of meeting logistics, ask for and give feedback on how things are working. If your protégé is not taking the lead like you wish he would, give him the feedback. Also, ask for feedback on whether you are being as available as the protégé would like. Make feedback a natural part of your mentoring conversations to build a stronger partnership. We will discuss feedback more in depth in the third rule of mentoring, Create a Safe Place.

Do Not Chase a Protégé

The advice in this chapter has focused on making it easy for the protégé to take the lead in the mentoring partnership. As noted earlier, the mentor is in the natural position to lead. You are working against these forces to make the path to leading easier for the protégé. The truth is, even if you do everything right to set the tone and get the meetings started, you may still have a protégé who is not engaged with mentoring. You and your protégé could be facing an issue of bad timing, competing priorities, or weak motivation. Sometimes there is a lack of interpersonal chemistry between the partners, but those cases are infrequent. Whatever the case, you may have a partnership that will not get off the ground at this time.

In these cases, it is best not to chase the protégé. Mentoring is a gift to be shared with someone who is ready to receive it. You cannot force mentoring on an unwilling protégé. What you can do is reach out from time to time to extend the offer again. You may find that circumstances change

Lead by Following   29

and the protégé is in a position to engage again. In this case, you may need to help a protégé overcome some embarrassment from not engaging sooner. Reassure him that the time is not always right for mentoring and that you are willing to help whenever it is.

On the other hand, you may find that this protégé will never be interested in mentoring from you. There are two key points to remember in this case. First, do not take it personally. Experience has taught me that, in the majority of cases, it is not an issue with the mentor that keeps mentoring from taking off. Typically, something else has taken precedence with the protégé and he is not able to prioritize mentoring. As a result, you also should not hold a grudge if you feel your mentoring is being rejected. You are better off not mentoring an uninterested protégé than trying to mentor one who is there only to prevent themselves from disappointing you.

The second point is to look for other protégés for whom the timing is better. Just as I tell protégés that they may have to talk to several prospective mentors before they find one willing to make the time, you may have to offer mentoring to several protégés before you find one who is willing to do the work. Do not let one rejection keep you from sharing the gift you have.

Recognize Your Tendencies

As you can see, you may have to lay the groundwork for your protégé to take the lead. Once she does, however, you want to be mindful of your temptation to take the lead back. Get to know your own tendencies to take over and work to curb them when they start to emerge. Below are some of the tendencies that can undermine a protégé leading.

Filling the silence. Many of us are uncomfortable with pauses in the conversation. Our natural inclination is to fill the silence, which causes us to speak when the protégé has stopped. When you do this, you begin to take over the conversation from the protégé. If you hit a spot of silence, wait until you notice the silence and it has made you a little uncomfortable. Then, count slowly to ten in your head. More often than not, the protégé will start talking again, keeping the lead of the conversation.

Taking over the discussion. As mentioned earlier, a lot of us like solving problems, and a protégé can be a great source of interesting problems to solve. They can be especially interesting because we are not directly involved in the issue, so we have the luxury of a third-party, almost academic perspective. There are many telltale signs that let you know you are taking over:

- You are doing more of the talking during your discussions than the protégé.
- You are generating more of the ideas for solutions than the protégé.
- You are devoting more time between mentoring sessions working on the issue than the protégé.

30   *Lead by Following*

When you find yourself in one of these patterns, use it as a signal that you want to take a step back and reinforce the protégé's role leading the discussion. A later mentoring rule, Good Questions Beat Good Advice, will help you use questions to redirect the ownership of the discussion to the protégé.

Asking advice-laden questions. Another habit you want to watch out for is delivering advice in the form of a question, for example, "Have you thought about creating a team charter to outline goals and responsibilities?" or "Do you think giving your peer direct feedback would help?" Both of these questions are really your thoughts on how to solve the problem. While a few questions like these can help a protégé explore other options, if the majority of your questions are of this variety, you are likely doing more of the problem solving than your protégé. If you catch yourself asking several leading questions, switch to more open-ended questions, sometimes as simple as, "What have you tried so far?" or "When you have been in situations like this in the past, how did you handle it?"

Directing the protégé's goals. One more sign that you are taking the lead is when you start to heavily influence the goals the protégé has for herself. This trap is easy to fall into because many protégés come to mentoring with relatively modest goals. They aren't thinking about their long-term future when they come to mentoring, and may be bringing you more tactical, immediate problems to solve. I made this mistake with one of my own protégés. He came to mentoring seeking advice on how to grow into his role as a leadership development professional. While that conversation was important, I saw what seemed like a larger gap in terms of long-term career direction. I asked him to conduct some career discovery exercises to explore different options. While he willingly did them, it became apparent that his focus was more on getting comfortable in his current position and that the long-term discussion was not what he needed at the time.

As soon as you start overriding your protégé's goals, you sap the energy and drive from those goals provided by the protégé. When you take a more active leadership role in setting goals for the protégé, you run the risk of draining the motivation that brought your protégé to mentoring in the first place. In the next chapter, we will explore how to chart a course with a protégé and keep the ownership of the goals with her.

These tendencies are meant to be signposts to let you know that you may be taking over leadership from the protégé. Filling silence or asking an advice-laden question from time to time will not immediately derail mentoring. But, paying attention to when you are doing them more often can be an early sign that you are taking the lead in the partnership. When any of these things happen, take a step back and remind yourself that you are here to lead by following, which will enable a more powerful mentoring partnership.

Checklist to Lead by Following

Use the checklist below to help your protégé take the lead in your partnership:

- Give permission to the protégé to ask for time on your calendar.
- Tell the protégé the easiest way to schedule (and reschedule) meetings with you.
- Spend time getting to know your protégé to build trust and break down power distance.
- Suggest a meeting schedule that will accommodate your availability and the protégé's needs.
- Reach out to a protégé if meetings become sporadic, but do not chase the protégé.

Reference

Horowitz, B. (2014). *The Hard Thing about Hard Things*. HarperBusiness.

3   Chart a Course

"I know this problem seems very important right now, but is this what you and I should be spending our time talking about?"

Mitch's mouth hung open for a minute as he looked at his mentor in stunned silence. His first thought was, Of course we should talk about this! *He felt his face turning flush, staring at his mentor as if she were his mother scolding him. Before he could speak, Sahira, his mentor, continued. "I didn't mean to cut you off like that, but it seems like we have spent the last two meetings talking about your frustration with the account representative selling clients things you can't deliver. I admit that is an important topic, but I thought the goal of our meetings was helping you learn more about the marketing organization."*

Mitch's mind raced as he was transported back to five months ago, his first meeting with Sahira. Her office was located in the labyrinth of hallways and cubicles on the seventeenth floor, and he got lost looking for it the first time he visited her. The marketing department could be an imposing place for outsiders, especially for someone from project management like Mitch. Everyone walked a little faster and was dressed a little better than those who worked on Mitch's floor. He had signed up for the company's mentoring program to learn more about the marketing organization and to see if he wanted to move his career in that direction. At that meeting, they laid out a six-month plan for Mitch to meet managers in different marketing groups, attend meetings with Sahira, and decide if marketing felt like a fit for him. Mitch left that meeting feeling elated with a new sense of hope.

*That was five months ago. Since then, Mitch has been swamped managing a project that keeps eating up more of his time. He is feeling battered from all sides, with his boss telling him he needs to manage the margin on his project better, and sales telling him he needs to speed things up to meet the client's needs. His meeting last week with the account representative got his blood boiling. It ended with Mitch slamming his fist on the table and saying, "You have **got** to stop promising the client things we can't deliver! We are losing money on this project!" Now, he is staring at his mentor, who is questioning whether they should be spending time on the most important issue he is facing today!*

Sahira is an experienced mentor, and she is well versed in the rules of mentoring. She invested the time during their early meetings to really understand Mitch's goals for mentoring to prepare for this exact moment. She knows that the best mentoring partnerships start at Rule #2: Chart a Course.

The future-oriented focus of mentoring is part of what separates the mentor's role from that of boss, coach, advisor, or other relationships you might have in your work career. While these other roles do not preclude spending time talking about the future, a mentor can create time and space for you to think beyond your current situation, to envision a future for yourself, and to discover a path to get there. Because mentors are more experienced than protégés, they have a perspective that can inform and shape a protégé's thinking on longer-term issues that others cannot provide. In addition, most mentors are not typically involved directly in the protégé's situation, so they can provide the third-party distance that creates a safe, objective space.

That is not to say a mentor cannot engage in the tactical conversation of a coach. In fact, there can be a lot of coaching that goes on in a mentoring partnership. Sahira could spend time talking to Mitch about his challenges with the sales organization or how to talk to his boss about the situation. In fact, she had already spent two meetings on that topic. At the same time, she saw Mitch's original goal slipping into the background as he became consumed with the immediacy of his situation. Her question was not meant to be disrespectful of Mitch or to belittle his predicament. In fact, she asked it as a question to allow for the possibility that Mitch wanted advice on this issue before returning to his larger goal.

But, she also wanted to throw Mitch a lifeline. He was sinking into the morass of his current reality and losing sight of his larger goals. Worse, he was letting an opportunity to start moving forward with his career exploration slip away as he expended time and energy with his mentor talking about the troubles of today. That is precisely why spending time on understanding a protégé's larger journey pays off. It would be easy for Sahira to get sucked into Mitch's situation and devote all of their time to it, knowing that Mitch was not going to be able to change the culture that existed between sales and project management. By understanding his goals, she is able to pull him up from his quagmire to give him the time to think about his future.

The Journey Provides Direction and Energy

Mitch and Sahira had built a trusting partnership over the course of five months. He has come to see their meetings as a safe place where he can talk about whatever was on his mind. Therefore, it is natural and normal for him to want to vent about the issues he was having at work. She had

34   *Chart a Course*

proven to be a sympathetic ear, and he valued her advice and insight. The question Mitch was not asking himself is, "Is this the best use of my time with my mentor?"

When Mitch and Sahira began working together, he had a clear goal in mind: He wanted to explore a career path in marketing, which was a natural fit for his role. What he also needed was some time and space to explore these future roles. Like most of us, Mitch had a demanding job where taking time out to explore the future is a luxury. The meetings with Sahira were safe from the distractions of his current reality to give him the freedom needed to truly think, ponder, and explore. While we should not blame Mitch for allowing his daily role back in, we must also recognize that he is sacrificing the time he could be spending on the future to deal with the present. In fact, he is probably not accustomed to having such time set aside, and the stress of his current situation is causing him to lose sight of his larger goals.

Sahira started the process by having Mitch talk about his long-term goals for exactly this moment. She wanted to understand the larger journey he is on, both where he had been and where he wanted to go. By exploring his journey together, they both understood his larger career context. They spent time talking about his longer-term career goals and used the goals to set a direction for their conversations. From there, they explored a variety of topics and issues on that larger career path to further Mitch's learning.

In addition to providing direction for the partnership, exploring the journey and charting a course forward helps the protégé tap into the energy needed to sustain a mentoring partnership. To have a mentoring partnership go beyond the first few meetings, a protégé needs to prioritize time spent with you over every other way she could spend her time. In fact, since she is in the driver's seat with your partnership, her time with you may feel like the only area where she has any discretion, which puts mentoring into competition with a lot of other demands.

Every day, you make hundreds if not thousands of choices of how to spend your time. You make most of those choices without thinking. An email comes in from your boss, and you hit "Reply" and start composing a response without thinking, *Do I need to reply to this right now?* An alert goes off that tells you you have a meeting in ten minutes, and you gather what you will need and head off to the meeting without asking yourself, *Is this meeting the best way to spend the next hour?*

The time your protégé spends with you is competing with all of these demands on her time, meaning that it is vulnerable to being pushed aside by these demands unless the protégé prioritizes mentoring over the other demands. One way to push mentoring time up on her priority list is to make it a net positive energy source. The effort and energy needed to push aside the other demands need to be outweighed by the energy she draws from the time spent with you.

Mentoring energy comes from several different sources. The first is the strength of the interpersonal bond the two of you feel. If your protégé likes you and likes spending time with you, she will draw energy from that time. However, the energy from the interpersonal bond may not be enough in the face of the other demands. Charting a course with a protégé helps tap into some of these other sources.

When thinking about the future, many protégés can be fueled by the **optimism** that comes from the discussion. The future is full of possibilities and opportunities, which can generate excitement for a protégé. The discussions can also fuel a protégé's **ambition** for her future. She may draw energy from working toward meaningful goals and making tangible progress. Finally, talking about the future can give a protégé some **sense of control** over her destiny. Having a safe place to think about something beyond today may give her respite from the weight of the demands placed on her today.

Spending time early on talking about the protégé's goals and aspirations for the future prepares you and your protégé to sustain your partnership through challenging times. When your protégé starts to become overwhelmed with a current problem, ask the question that Sahira did at the beginning: would our time be better spent on the current issue or returning to our larger goals? If the protégé wants to spend the time on the current situation, there may still be ways for you to use the protégé's journey to see the larger context surrounding the issue. After the situation has calmed down, you can encourage your protégé to reassess her journey: given what happened, do you see your path forward changing? Or, was the challenge temporary and is the protégé ready to resume talking about the original goals?

Having a mentor as an ally during difficulties can be like a lighthouse in a storm. By being there to provide steady support, you will help the protégé navigate challenges while at the same time strengthening your partnership. Spending time up front talking about goals and the protégé's future enables you to play this role.

Looking Back over the Journey

When you start talking about future hopes and ambitions, some protégés can launch into a goal-setting process without much trouble. Many will find the process energizing and take on the task with a lot of enthusiasm. Other protégés, however, find the goal-setting process stressful and intimidating. Many of them do not spend much time thinking about the future in a tangible sense. The question, "Where do you see yourself in three or four years?" is met with nervous laughter or embarrassment that she has not devoted much time to thinking about it. You may want to reassure your protégé that you don't spend a lot of time thinking about it either and not to worry about it.

36   *Chart a Course*

To take the stress out of a forward-looking goal-setting process, it can be helpful to start by reflecting on the past. If the protégé is truly on a long-term journey, you may want to look over where the journey has gone over the last few years. The reflection exercise takes pressure off the protégé, since she should feel much more comfortable talking about the recent journey. The reflection also helps you understand the protégé's larger context of her journey and draw insights about where her path has taken her.

To help get the conversation started, it may help for you to complete the exercise yourself. As you answer the questions below, you may start to empathize with your protégé about the level of effort it takes to think about these topics. Set aside fifteen or so minutes where you won't have too many distractions, and answer the questions below. As with the other exercises in this book, don't just put down short, one-word answers. Truly reflect on the question and think about what it is asking you.

1. Where were you on your career journey two years ago? Where did that version of you think you would be today? How similar or different is where you are today from where you envisioned you would be?

2. How have you grown or changed over the last two years? What are you better at than you were before? What new things have you learned that you may still be working on? What important lessons have you learned that had an impact on who you are today?

3. If you were to ask someone close to you how you are different from how you were two years ago, what would she or he say? What evidence would they point to of how you are different?

4. As you think about the journey that led you to where you ended up (versus where you thought you would), how much of your journey was truly planned versus luck or good/bad fortune? What role has

serendipity played in your journey? What help did you get from others along the way?

5. How easy was it for you to answer these questions? Which gave you the most trouble? What insights can you draw about your recent journey that help you think about the road ahead?

Taking stock of the last few years with questions like these can help you see the larger landscape of your journey better. It is meant to free you from the constraints of what you are facing at present and put you in the mindset of growth, learning, and possibility. If you can think about where you have been, you can start to project forward to where you want to go. In fact, the start of the goal-setting process is to take the first three questions, but start them with, "It is two years from now ..."

These questions are a tool to use with your protégé. Set aside time to talk about these questions. You may even send the questions in advance to let your protégé think about them. They can be a great warmup for the next exercise of setting goals. Before you do that, make sure you answer the questions yourself. Put yourself in your protégé's shoes to experience what answering these questions feels like. Use that empathy to encourage your protégé to explore her own journey.

Phases of Career Exploration

To ease the transition from looking backward to looking ahead, it can help to understand what phase the protégé has reached in his journey. If you return to the magic question, "Where do you want to be in five years?", the answer that comes back can indicate where the protégé is in exploring and navigating a career. Most protégés can be described as falling into one of the following four phases of exploration: Explorer, Scout, Navigator, and Homesteader. When discussing these phases with your protégé, it helps to establish a time frame, as the answer may be different if you are thinking twelve months versus five years. Asking a protégé to think about three years from now is usually a time frame that seems far enough into the future to hold possibilities without being so far in the future to lose tangible meaning.

38 *Chart a Course*

Explorer

The first phase of career exploration starts with exploration. The Explorer is the protégé who has a burning desire for something. She yearns for a future full of possibility, but isn't sure what that future looks like or what is even possible. She brings the drive and enthusiasm of learning. She wants to know where she can take herself, what will be fulfilling for her. The future looks like endless opportunity, which carries with it the overwhelming prospect of too many choices.

The Explorer comes to mentoring wanting to try things out. She wants to test paths to see where they could go and learn what will be right for her. For her, mentoring can be like a survey course to a career. She wants to sample all of the possibilities before pursing one. She wants to connect with people who can answer her questions and start to chart her own course.

While many young protégés find themselves standing here at the start of a long career, the Explorer is also the domain of many mid-career protégés. They may have been on a course of someone else's making until they reach the top of the first ladder, not knowing where the next ladder starts. Brian was one such Explorer. He had climbed the marketing career ladder of a multinational consumer products company until he reached the pinnacle: senior brand director of one of the company's most prestigious brands. The problem was, he was only thirty-nine; there was no discernible next step for him. He was just as much an Explorer as the twenty-two-year-old who just started with the company.

As a mentor, you can help a protégé at this stage by helping with the exploration. Spend time teaching her about the larger organization or profession to help her see possibilities. Connect her with people in your network who can help her explore. Brainstorm questions she can ask herself or others about what is possible. The primary goal for an Explorer often is to start to find a direction to her career by exploring and narrowing down possibilities.

Do not rush an Explorer through this stage too quickly. Some Explorers enjoy seeing nothing but opportunity and possibility ahead of them. But, many are uncomfortable exploring because they think they need to have a direction and a goal set. Part of your job is to remind her that it is okay to spend time exploring and that she should not settle for the first opportunity that comes along. Help her be comfortable with the magic question being unanswered for a while. The process of exploring can take months (sometimes years). Part of what she is doing is ruling out paths that she does not want to pursue as much as selecting a path that she does.

Scout

While Explorers are in search of a direction for themselves, other protégés approach mentoring with a goal in mind. They have surveyed the map and have selected a destination for themselves. What the Scout wants is a path to his goal. He knows where he's heading, but he isn't sure the best path to get there. Many Scouts come around to the notion that good work does *not* necessarily speak for itself and that good things do *not* always come to those who wait. The Scout wants to take an active role in moving himself toward his goals, but is not sure what path will get him there.

Julio was a forty-two-year-old manager in an apparel manufacturer who wanted to move into the executive ranks in five to seven years, but was faced with too many options for moving ahead. Should he take an international assignment to get experience with the company's overseas operations? Should he pursue an MBA at a prestigious university? Will spending time in the company's Emerging Leaders program help him advance? He knew the direction he wanted to take, but was searching for the path to get there.

The Scout approaches mentoring with two basic needs. First, he wants to know if he has chosen the right destination for himself. As a mentor, you can "pressure-test" the Scout's chosen destination. Ask questions like, What interests you about that goal? What makes you a good fit for that goal? You have no doubt seen people who set a goal around a job title without thinking through what that job would entail or whether it fits with their strengths and interests. When asking these questions, you are not trying to talk your protégé out of his objectives. Rather, you are helping him examine the goal from a rational place. Sometimes the Scout talks himself out of a goal. But, more often, he becomes more confident that the goal is worth pursuing, and may create additional energy for pursuing it.

Only after the protégé has answered these questions can he and his mentor work on the second part: How does he get there? It is here that the mentor can rely on years of experience to help a protégé to find the right path. Mentoring can then focus on crafting the right path for the protégé and initiating the first steps. Brainstorm together different tactics the protégé can use to start making progress. Focus on some short-term wins that can help the protégé feel some forward progress that can create momentum. Some Scouts will want to put together a plan that maps out the next several years. Others will want to map out six to twelve months at a time. Once they have accomplished those steps, they will want to plan the next six to twelve months. When helping a Scout plan, keep in mind the first rule: Lead by Following. Let your protégé guide what sorts of goals he sets. You can challenge and push your protégé, but be sensitive to resistance that tells you that you may be taking over the lead.

Navigator

The third phase of exploration can be confusing to a mentor. The Navigator approaches mentoring with a goal in mind and a course laid out. As the mentor, you might ask, "You seem to have it figured out. Do

40   *Chart a Course*

you really need my help?" Yet, the protégé in the Navigator phase needs the mentor just as much as in the prior phases. She may have a path laid out, but she wants someone along for the journey.

Elise was a project engineer for an engineering consulting firm. She knew that she was headed toward the ranks of principal in the next five years. She also knew that she needed to successfully lead larger and more complex projects to be competitive for that role. However, she quickly learned that knowing the course and traversing it were not the same thing. She wanted a guide to be alongside her to keep her moving in the right direction and helping her over obstacles as she encountered them.

Just like with Scouts, spend a little time pressure testing the Navigator's goals. Use similar questions to see if the destination is really what the protégé thinks it is. Nothing is more disappointing than spending years in pursuit of a goal only to achieve it and realize it never was what you wanted to do. Think of the young physician, lawyer, or engineer who pushed through college and graduate school only to realize three years into the job that he had been pursuing his parents' goal the whole time. Do not let a robust career plan fool you into thinking the protégé has asked himself these questions. Spend some time asking the questions and getting a better understanding of the Navigator's goals in pursuing them.

Once you have examined the goals with the protégé, you will find that helping a Navigator can be a lot like being a personal trainer at the gym. The Navigator knows she needs to work out because it is on her plan, and even knows what to do at the gym. However, when the alarm goes off at 5:00 a.m., it is a lot easier to get out of bed when she knows her trainer will be waiting for her when she gets there. Navigators need someone to create subtle accountability to do what they know they need to do. Simply asking about what progress she has made on her plan creates a subtle pull that helps her do what she knows she needs to do. In addition to creating accountability, you can also help with unexpected setbacks as well as being a cheering section when they reach milestones. Working with a Navigator can be very satisfying since you often can see tangible progress sooner than with other protégés.

Homesteader

The protégé who reaches the fourth phase of exploration has arrived at his destination. He is where he wants to be for the foreseeable future, often focusing on his current role and being the best he can be at it. When asked, "Where do you want to be in three years?", the answer comes back, "Where I am today." Do not assume that Homesteaders lack ambition or drive. In fact, the reverse is often the case: he wants to learn as much as he can about his current role and do it well. In fact, this role may be the one for which he has been preparing for a while. He wants to learn about his role and how it fits into the organization. He wants to

Chart a Course 41

continue to grow in his role lest he become stagnant. He is not thinking about the next opportunity right now. Rather, he wants to keep growing where he is. At the end of the day, if we are honest with ourselves, most of us are probably Homesteaders in our roles. We are not focused on where we want to go next; we want to enjoy what we are doing now.

Ian was the ideal Homesteader. He had just been promoted to project manager for a pharmaceutical company in the discovery R&D group. Being a project manager was a lot different than being a bench chemist, and he had a lot to learn about leading people and managing a complex project. The next role would be five years off at best, and would likely require relocating the the company's headquarters. His partner had a great job and his kids were in middle school. All signs pointed to him working in his current role for a while.

But, as a Homesteader, Ian didn't want to settle in and get too comfortable. He didn't want this job to be his last by default. He wanted to keep his career development alive. The Homesteader wants to keep learning and growing, deepening his understanding of how he can contribute to the organization. He also wants to keep options open for the future; he may not be looking for the next role today, but is open to looking at opportunities that come his way. As Louis Pasteur said, "Chance only favors the mind which is prepared." Think about the times that a great opportunity found you. How would it have felt if the perfect opportunity came to you and you were not ready for it?

> Chance only favors the mind which is prepared.
> —Louis Pasteur

As a mentor, you have an opportunity to help the Homesteader see how the larger organization works and where the protégé fits into it. You can help him find new ways to contribute and expand his role, creating learning opportunities along the way. You can explore his strengths and weaknesses in his current role and help find ways to achieve excellence where he is.

Disorderly Progression

After reading the prior descriptions, you may think your protégé will follow a neat course of progressing from Explorer to Scout to Navigator to Homesteader. While the phases are laid out as a logical progression, most protégés do not experience them in order. Reflect again on your own crooked path. If you think about how your own journey unfolded, you will realize that careers rarely follow an orderly trajectory. Your protégé will likely spend time in more than one phase as he actively explores his journey with you. Some Explorers jump to Navigator once they have found their chosen path; they quickly chart a course and begin down it. Some Scouts and Navigators switch to being Explorers once they start going down a path and start to feel like it is not right for them or as circumstances change.

42   *Chart a Course*

As a mentor, one of your greatest gifts is your flexibility. As your protégé moves through the phases, you can adapt to meet your protégé's needs, changing the focus of your mentoring to match the needs of your protégé. Every once in a while, ask about your protégé's phase of exploration. Her focus may have changed without even thinking about it. Acknowledging the change in exploration can help you adjust how the two of you work together.

Exploration as Both Phase and Type

One thing I have learned since first introducing this typology to protégés is that many of them describe themselves as having a foot in two different phases: "I'm a Homesteader who is also Exploring." At first, it seemed like they were thinking in two different time frames, identifying as a Homesteader in the near term but an Explorer in the long term. What has become apparent is, in addition to describing a process of exploration, the four phases also describe different types of approaches to career navigation overall. Some of us identify most naturally with one of the four phases as a type. As you read the descriptions above, you may have gravitated to one of them not because it represents where you are today but how you approach your journey overall. This point is worth noting to help you better understand your protégé's type and phase.

When approaching careers, the Explorer types are always curious and exploring other opportunities. They are looking for new experiences and looking for new things to learn. In fact, their challenge may be one of focus: you cannot effectively pursue three goals at the same time. The Scout type is someone who doesn't put together multi-year plans. She prefers to plan out the next few months, execute that plan, and then plan the subsequent few months. The Navigator type is someone who is very comfortable with multi-year plans and feels uncomfortable when things are up in the air (a more natural state for Explorers and some Scouts). Finally, the Homesteader type is someone who likes to go deep on one thing (in contrast with the Explorer, who likes to go wide). She challenges herself to achieve excellence at what she is doing.

You can help your protégé by separating his type from his phase and helping him get comfortable with the phase. An Explorer type may be uncomfortable making plans, but may need someone help him through the Scout or Navigator phases to keep him from spinning his wheels with exploring. Conversely, a Navigator type may need to get comfortable with the Explorer phase, where there are multiple paths that need to be explored. You can help her overcome the temptation of selecting the first path and planning it out.

In the end, the four phases are meant to give you an idea of where the protégé is in his journey. More importantly, it gets the protégé to think about his future direction in a way he may not have done before. The

Chart a Course   43

goal of discussing the phases is not to arrive at a precise definition of the protégé's phase so much as to help the two of you understand where he is in terms of career exploration.

Charting a Course for Mentoring

To this point, we have considered the path behind the protégé and how the protégé is thinking about the future. These steps are meant to prepare you and your protégé for the next conversations: Where does the protégé want to go, and how can you, as a mentor, help with the journey? You could easily skip this step and just start talking about whatever issues are interesting to the protégé right now. What you will miss by not talking about the larger journey is direction and context. For example, your protégé might want to talk about how to handle conflict with a peer. While you could jump into this topic and have a great conversation, you would be missing several things:

1. Why is this topic interesting or important to the protégé?
2. Is the issue with this particular coworker, or does the protégé struggle with conflict in general?
3. Is the protégé's capability in handling conflict creating larger challenges, such being overworked because he cannot say "no" to people?

Without the larger context, you may still have a productive discussion around conflict with this particular coworker, but you will miss the power that mentoring holds. Just as Mitch and Sahira at the beginning of the chapter could have had a good discussion about his challenges with the sales team, he would have missed the opportunity to tap into the wealth of her knowledge and experience.

Set aside some time to talk through the protégé's overall career goals and what the two of you want to focus on in your conversations. Many protégés get stuck at this step because they want to have precisely measurable goals, especially when they are in a formal mentoring program. Follow the four steps below and make the process conversational. If you can get the conversation flowing, you should end up with a direction for your partnership.

Step 1: Talk About the Future

Start the conversation with the magic question: "Where do you want to be in three to five years?" In fact, you may want to ask your protégé to think about the question before the two of you discuss it. Letting the protégé have some time to think about the answer beforehand can take off some of the pressure of having to come up with it on the spot when talking with you. After the magic question, you can use the questions

44   *Chart a Course*

below to guide the conversation. Or, you can send them in advance and then review your protégé's thoughts:

- What kind of work do you want to be doing?
- How much will your role involve leading people, if at all?
- In what geography do you want to be working?
- At what company (or type of company) do you want to be?

Scouts and Navigators can sometimes answer these questions easily. They may have already given it a fair amount of thought. Homesteaders, however, may feel a little deflated since they likely want to be in the same role at the same company. For them, ask them probing questions, such as:

- What would an ideal version of your job look like?
- What would you change about your job if you could? What would you do more of or less of?
- What about your job is most interesting? What would it look like if you could focus on that more?
- What part of your job is least interesting? What would you have to do to minimize that part of the role?

Explorers may also struggle with giving specific answers to the two sets of questions, but they may be able to speak more generally about their interests. If your protégé is an Explorer, make sure he feels comfortable saying, "I don't know." Let him know that you are looking forward to discovering some of the answers together.

Step 2: Talk about Today

Once you have talked about future goals, bring the conversation around to today. You may have heard the term SWOT analysis in the context of setting company strategy; talk to your protégé about conducting a SWOT analysis on his career. The term SWOT is an acronym, which stands for Strengths, Weaknesses, Opportunities, and Threats. It is a useful tool for describing the current state facing a protégé.

- **Strengths.** What assets does the protégé have that will make it easier for him to achieve his longer-term career objectives? These assets can be education or training, work experiences, certifications, or personal qualities such as communication or organization skills.
- **Weaknesses.** What are the protégé's liabilities relative to his goals? What qualities or attributes may keep him from achieving his goals? These liabilities can be the flip side of the strengths above, such as *lack of* certain education or work experience. They also can be personal qualities like being argumentative or disorganized that can hold him back.

The Strengths/Weaknesses part of the conversation can be very enlightening for you, and a chance for the protégé to reflect on where he is today. The Weaknesses part of the conversation may be difficult if the protégé is embarrassed by some of his liabilities. You may be able to make that part of the conversation easier by talking about some of your own weaknesses and help the protégé feel comfortable sharing his with you.

- **Opportunities.** What are the paths the protégé can take that will help him achieve his goal? These may be training or tuition reimbursement the company offers or job assignments he can request. It may also include growth in a profession or department that will create opportunities for the protégé to pursue.
- **Threats.** What are the barriers in the protégé's path that could impede his progress toward his goals? Threats may include lack of jobs in a department in which the protégé is interested or cutbacks to programs that would have helped the protégé make progress. It could include job or other requirements, such as a certain educational degree or certification, that the protégé does not possess.

In short, Opportunities are anything that will make the protégé's journey easier, and Threats are anything that will make the journey harder. You may be able to help the protégé think through this part of the conversation, as you may have a broader perspective that can help the protégé see things he may be missing. You can also help evaluate the size of the Opportunities or Threats in a way that helps the protégé see them in the most realistic light.

Step 3: Talk about the Plan

After talking through the destination (Step 1) and the starting point (Step 2), you can ask what is the protégé's plan for her journey. It is at this point that you can see the difference between Scouts and Navigators. The Navigator will be able to articulate many steps she is planning to take over the next few years. She may even provide a high degree of detail to the steps, with some steps even having sub-steps to them. A Scout, on the other hand, may only have a few steps in mind, and they may be fairly high level. Your goal in asking the question is not to judge the protégé's plan but to understand what she has in mind. You should ask questions to probe and understand the plan overall as well as the steps contained within it:

- What steps have you started already? What progress have you made?
- What is important about a particular step in the plan? How does it help you get closer to your goals?
- When do you see yourself completing the steps? What sort of timing are you looking at?
- What steps did you consider, but leave off? What caused you to drop them?

46   *Chart a Course*

Step 4: Talk about a Focus for Mentoring

Now that you have talked through the intended journey, ask the question, "How can I help you? What can you and I work on together that will help you?" If the two of you have taken the time to think through the prior four steps, you will likely find the topics will come easily. Be sure to remember the first rule at this point: Lead by Following. Let the protégé tell you what he would like to talk about first. You may have some ideas of goals the two of you could set for mentoring, but you want to be mindful of taking over. Choosing the focus for your conversations is a critical step, and you want to make sure your protégé is still setting the direction. Below are some sample goals to get your protégé started.

Explorer Goals:

- Learn more about my mentor's function within the organization and how it relates to my own.
- Meet with senior leaders in the finance function to see what career paths are available.

Scout Goals:

- Build a three-year career plan for moving to a management role with detailed action steps.
- Investigate options for moving to the next level, including internal training options, a local MBA program, and external leadership opportunities.

Navigator Goals:

- As part of my four-year plan, execute the following steps:
  - Enroll in supervisory skills training.
  - Visit our R&D facility to understand how their work integrates with marketing.

Homesteader Goals:

- Take on additional responsibilities in addition to my current role; ask my boss to delegate some of her tasks to me.
- Volunteer to lead a cross-functional project to better understand how my work supports the organization's strategy.

Jump-starting the Conversation

You may find that your protégé is not ready for the larger conversation of his career journey. He has come to you for some advice, and may find a conversation about his future intimidating. It may also be that he doesn't know you very well yet, and may not be ready to have a deeper conversation about the future before knowing whether he believes you will be able to help.

Whatever the case, it can be helpful to set aside the conversation about the protégé's journey and just start a conversation. You can learn a lot about your protégé by talking through one of the topics below, and she can learn about you and how you might be able to help her. Use the list below to jump-start a conversation. Ask your protégé to review the list and select one or two topics to use as a starting place:

Communication and listening skills	Time management
Customer partnerships (internal or external)	Personal productivity
	Project management
Self-confidence	Meeting effectiveness
Strategic thinking	Building a team
Setting direction	Achieving work/life balance
Creating a vision	Influencing others
Motivating others	Stress management
Delegation/empowerment	Setting goals
Developing others	Improving reporting relationships
Conflict management	Learning better people management
Performance issues	Understanding company politics
Negotiation skills	Enhancing organizational visibility.

Once she has selected a topic, start with the question, "What about that topic is interesting to you?" You can then start exploring the topic together, sharing your ideas and experiences while also learning about your protégé. You can always return to the larger question of the protégé's journey when you feel like your protégé is ready to talk about it.

Keeping on Course

As Mitch and Sahira saw at the beginning of the chapter, it is very easy for mentoring partners to lose sight of their larger goals. Protégés may not be accustomed to the future-oriented conversations. While they may be engaging at first, it takes a lot of energy to keep up focus on goals that are years into the future. Present realities can often creep into the mentoring conversation, especially as the trust begins to build between mentor and protégé. Mitch's current situation with the account representative was a hot issue for him and he has found a sympathetic ear where he can vent. As you will see in an upcoming chapter, part of Sahira's role is to create a safe place where Mitch can share his frustrations. But, she also owes it to Mitch to encourage him to use his time with her looking past the account representative to his larger goals.

48   *Chart a Course*

When your conversations with your protégé start to drift away from larger goals to focus on present concerns, use the following phrases to share that feedback:

> "I notice that our last few conversations have focused on some of your short-term issues. While I want you to have a place to share those, I'm wondering if our time is better spent on those issues for now, or if you wanted to return to the goals we set earlier."

Note that the feedback says, "our last few conversations ..." You do not want to redirect the conversation the moment things drift into current challenges. Also, you want to leave the door open to spending more time on the issues. Be prepared for the conversation to go into one of the following directions.

Spend Time Here

It may be that your protégé wants to devote some more mentoring time to the present challenges. You may be the only safe place he has to share these concerns. **Slower is faster.** He may have been holding onto these issues for a while and needs somewhere to blow off a little steam. You can offer to spend some of the mentoring time on these issues and start building in the longer-term goals in the conversations over the next few meetings.

There is one thing to keep an eye on: getting drawn into the issues yourself. Many mentors sympathize with the struggle the protégé is facing and want to take some action or play a more active role than just advisor. As was mentioned in the prior chapter, trying to fix the protégé's problems robs him of learning opportunities and has the possibility of creating dependence. The rule of thumb mentors follow is, unless there is something illegal or unethical going on that threatens real harm to the protégé, others, or the organization, it is best to stay in the advisor role and to have patience. Remember that slower is faster, and you may have to allow your protégé to go through the struggle at her pace.

Return to the Goals

When you hold up the mirror on your mentoring conversations, your protégé may realize that time with a mentor is precious and she may want to return to the goals that brought her to mentoring. Assure her that you can still discuss the current issues if she needs to, but allow her to take the conversation back to the more strategic discussion of her longer path of exploration. You can ask about the issue in current meetings to leave the door open a little and let her know it is okay if she needs to get something off her chest in a safe place. But, let her guide the conversation back after your gentle feedback.

Prepare to Change Course

The third situation does not happen often, but you want to be aware if it does. The issue that is consuming your protégé might be the tip of an iceberg and represent a change in his current situation. It may be that forces around him are moving him into a new direction and that his original goals may need to reexamined in that light. There was a protégé in a mentoring program who was relocated *three times* in one year while he was in the mentoring program. His mentor hung in with him through each of the transitions until he got on his feet after the final move. After that, they spent time reexamining his original goals and charted a new course from there.

It may also be that your protégé underestimated the role his current reality was playing and that the longer-term goals were not as realistic as they sounded originally. It could be for Mitch that his struggles with the sales organization were becoming known and making him less attractive to those in marketing. He may need to spend time on his current situation and work through those issues before tackling his larger career trajectory.

4 Create a Safe Place

Dennis had always been a perplexing protégé for Tom. In their meetings, Dennis would sit on the edge of his chair and talk rapidly, quickly scrawling long notes as they talked. He would always thank Tom and say how great the meeting was. At the same time, Tom felt like there was a lot about Dennis he didn't know. Whenever Tom would ask about what Dennis wanted out of his career at the company, Dennis would go quiet, his eyes darting around the room, before he would brighten back up and switch topics quickly, usually to an article he had just read in the Harvard Business Review. *Dennis seemed to resist talking about longer-term career plans, leaving Tom to wonder why. He was about to get his answer.*

When Tom walked into the sparse conference room for his meeting, Dennis was already sitting at the table with a few sheets of paper in front of him, not the stack of notes and articles he usually brought. "What's going on?" Tom asked. Instead of sitting at the edge of the seat full of energy, Dennis was sitting quietly with his hands on the table and fingers drumming on top of the sheets of paper, which Tom could see were printed email messages. Dennis drew up in his seat, took a deep breath, and, staring at the table between them, told Tom that these were job offers from other companies. Dennis had been working with a recruiter and interviewing with several other companies. Now, he was faced with two solid offers.

As Dennis told the story, he spoke in slow, measured words and his eyes never left the table. He said that he felt like his career at the company had stalled. He saw the only path to promotion was through his boss's job, and his boss didn't look like he was going anywhere anytime soon. Tom studied Dennis's face as he told the story; he looked sheepish, almost apologetic, for having applied for these jobs, let alone having gone on interviews. He finished with, "I've been scared to tell anyone here I've been looking. In fact, I'm nervous telling you this now. I don't want to be disloyal to the company, but I wanted help deciding what to do. You're the only one I feel like I can trust since you're my mentor."

Create a Safe Place 51

Tom was now facing one of the most important rules of mentoring, Creating a Safe Place. How he handled this moment in the conversation after Dennis had taken such a big risk was going to have implications both for their mentoring partnership and for Dennis's career direction for the next ten years.

Along with a protégé's drive, the trust that develops between a mentor and protégé is a critical ingredient to the growth of a successful mentoring partnership. Whenever I interview participants at the end of a mentoring program, I often hear that trust is what fueled the development of the relationship and led to the protégé experiencing the success she or he attained. Trust in a mentoring partnership is not a given. It can take a while to build, and sometimes does not grow at all. This chapter will delve into the role trust plays in mentoring and explore ways that can accelerate its growth.

Defining Trust

If you look up "trust" in the dictionary, you'll find that it is a "firm belief in the reliability, truth, ability, or strength of someone or something." While a solid definition, it doesn't tell me much about the trust that grows within a mentoring partnership. Instead, it is important to consider what trust does for a protégé. If a protégé has a belief in her mentor's reliability, what does that mean for her? And, how does a mentor know if she is trusted? What evidence would a mentor have that a protégé's trust is growing?

The definition of trust that I prefer comes from psychology, which says **trust is the willingness to be vulnerable to another person.** This definition goes beyond a belief and looks to the protégé's behavior. Trust has formed when a protégé takes risks with her mentor that make her vulnerable. This vulnerability comes when a protégé admits she has fears, doubts, frustrations, hopes, and dreams, especially ones she does not normally share with anyone else. It is precisely these things that are the grist for the mentoring mill, the issues that a protégé needs the time and space to discuss, explore, and act upon.

> Trust is the willingness to be vulnerable to another person.

Everyone has hopes and fears, but most of us have ones we keep concealed from others. Exposing them could bring ridicule, manipulation, or attack. Even worse, they could bring dismissiveness and indifference, telling a protégé that her dreams are mundane and unimportant. It is these threats that cause us to bottle up these feelings, allowing them to grow and become sources of frustration, anger, and disappointment. Creating a safe place for exploring them and exposing them to the light of day can be illuminating for a protégé, removing debilitating roadblocks or tapping into the energy locked up within unrealized aspirations.

52 *Create a Safe Place*

Trust is the Foundation of Mentoring

Trust is the foundation for any relationship, but it is especially important for mentors and protégés. A mentoring relationship's strength is tied directly to the degree to which the protégé trusts the mentor to have her or his best interests at heart. The protégé needs to believe the mentor is on his side and cares about the things that are important to the protégé. In fact, the protégé needs to believe the mentor cares about him. When the protégé believes in the benign and caring intentions of the mentor, he is able to begin revealing those things that have been hidden from others. It is this "psychosocial support" that Kathy Kram described in her classic piece on mentoring, *Mentoring at Work* (1985). As the trust grows, the relationship becomes stronger, allowing the protégé to begin to reap the benefits of having a mentor.

> The most important thing any mentor does is create a safe place for the protégé.

Expressing Frustration

One of the more basic ways a protégé benefits from this trust is by having a place to vent frustrations she is experiencing at work. Pamela was a marketing director at a large consumer products company. After a long, successful career with the company, she felt like her much younger boss had put her out to pasture. She had been relegated to a smaller brand in the company's portfolio and was told, "We don't expect too much growth out of this brand. Just keep it going." Pamela grew the market share for her brand by 15% with no additional resources, in a year when the other brands saw only 1–3% growth. Her boss said that while Pamela's results were good, they were not "innovative" enough and that she wouldn't get moved to a more significant brand.

The only thing that kept Pamela from leaving the company was Alana, her mentor. Whenever Pamela had a meeting with her boss that would get her blood boiling, she reached out to Alana, who was a vice president in the company. Alana allowed Pamela to vent her frustrations, talk about fairness, and ask, "What does 'innovative' mean, anyway?? I don't know what he wants me to do differently!" Even though Alana knew Pamela's boss, she made sure Pamela understood that their conversations were confidential, and that she would take no action outside of the meetings based on what Pamela shared. By giving these reassurances, Alana was creating a safe place for Pamela.

Many protégés need a safe place to air their grievances. Some need the emotional release that comes with telling someone else what has been bottled up and eating away at them. Others need to know that they are not the only ones who have faced these challenges. Still others want

Create a Safe Place 53

someone else to tell them that they have the right to be upset. While there can be a danger of creating a place for a protégé to wallow in self-pity (see Chapter 6: Balance Empathy and Action), the best mentors don't shy away from strong emotions that, if left bottled up, will leak out in less productive ways.

Dealing with Difficult Situations

Often a protégé wants more than just to express frustration; he wants to do something about it. In the example at the beginning of the chapter, Dennis wasn't just looking for a place to talk about his dissatisfaction with his situation. He was faced with a decision and was moving toward action. Tom was playing the role of dispassionate outsider who could help Dennis evaluate the situation, understand his options (including ones Dennis hadn't considered), and decide on a course of action.

To make the conversation productive, Dennis needed to trust Tom enough to share his perspective without censoring anything (including his assessment of his boss's lack of promotability). He also needed to trust that Tom didn't have a real stake in the situation. Others who are close to Dennis might have an interest in the decision he made; his boss might rely on him and not want to lose him. The prospective employers want him to come work for them. While Tom does have an interest in keeping Dennis with the company, he showed that he had Dennis's interest at heart by exploring the other options without judgment or making Dennis feel disloyal for looking. When a protégé can have an honest conversation with a mentor whom he trusts, he will be more confident in the decision that results.

Moving Outside the "Comfort Zone"

Some of the most profound growth and learning occurs when we go beyond what is comfortable and venture into uncharted territory. Getting outside the comfort zone is exciting, scary, enlightening, frightening, and thrilling all at the same time. Mentors are companions for these journeys; the protégé isn't going into the unknown alone. The mentor can be a source of strength and encouragement, especially when trying new things that have a risk of failure. She can take away barriers (both real and perceived) that stand between us and learning. She also picks us up when we stumble in the dark, and helps us celebrate our successes.

In fact, failure is a large part of learning. The first steps out of your comfort zone are usually unsteady, and you are not likely to get it right the first time. You want to create a safe place where your protégé is not backing away from risks because of the threat of failing, but is rather trying new things and learning what does and does not work. Part of the

54 Create a Safe Place

safe place is to encourage the risk, help your protégé get comfortable with it, and process through the outcomes, good or bad.

Having a mentor does not guarantee someone will take the big leap into the unfamiliar. Some protégés are more focused on the here and now and aren't ready for the growth that comes from the risk of the new and different. But, a mentor can make it more likely that a protégé is able to go beyond the comfortable and stretch him or herself.

Challenging Assumptions

A mentor's role may be to help a protégé examine and challenge assumptions that may be holding the protégé in place. Many protégés find themselves holding onto beliefs about their situations that are no longer true, or may never have been true. For example, Julie was a supply chain manager for an apparel manufacturer. She knew that she wanted to move up to higher-level manager roles in her organization. One of the steps on her path as a Navigator was to pursue an MBA at a local university. No small undertaking, Julie was looking at several years of hard work ahead of her. Before she applied to the program, she had a talk with her mentor, Ben, who helped her see that few if any of the senior managers at the companies had an MBA. While having an MBA was not a detriment, he noted, it certainly wasn't the key to promotion that she had believed. Through several meetings, Ben and Julie discussed other options for her to pursue for her development that would be more beneficial to her career path than an MBA. By challenging the assumption Julie had, Ben saved her a lot of time and trouble, and was able to focus her on a path that would be more productive for her.

As a mentor, you want to challenge assumptions tactfully and show respect for a belief the protégé may have held for a long time. Many protégés, for example, hold onto the belief that good work should speak for itself, which leads to frustration when they see peers whom they *perceive* as not working as hard getting ahead. Imagine if a mentor dismissed that belief out of hand, perhaps by saying, "That is ridiculous. Everyone knows that to get noticed, you have to speak up." You can see that the protégé may feel embarrassed, foolish, angry, or disheartened. He may have been frustrated for years watching peers advance, but still held onto the belief. As a result, the trust you have built with the protégé may be damaged, with the protégé thinking, *My mentor doesn't understand me.*

When challenging assumptions, start with phrases like, "I understand why you believe that," "It makes sense that you would think that," or "I used to feel that way myself." Beginning this way validates that the belief was not irrational and that the protégé was not foolish for holding onto it. Then, use your own experience and examples to share an alternate way of seeing things that dismantles the assumption.

From there, you can help your protégé find a new way to think about his situation.

Of course, some beliefs will be very difficult to dislodge. They may be more central to a protégé's beliefs about the world in general or more ingrained in his identity. If you experience a lot of resistance when challenging the assumption, you may need to back off of the challenge for a while. The protégé may need time to consider your challenge and reflect on how it fits with his worldview before he is ready to talk about it again. Or, he may not be willing to let go of it at all. In those cases, you have to proceed with the assumption as a given and help the protégé find ways to work around it.

Build a Relationship for the Future

As discussed earlier, mentoring is so powerful because it is so flexible. A mentor adapts to meet the needs of the protégé *when* the protégé has the need. Sometimes, the greatest need may not occur until years down the road. Building a strong, trusting relationship with a protégé today may have its greatest payoff five or ten years from now when the need arises. You may get a call out of the blue when your protégé is facing a crisis or a career-changing decision that needs the perspective of a trusted advisor. Maintaining contact during periods of mentoring dormancy helps keep the trust alive for those times when a protégé really needs it.

How Trust Grows

Trust is the currency of mentoring. We all have "trust accounts" with those around us. Some have larger deposits with us than others, allowing us to trust them more. The more trust a protégé has **Trust is the currency of mentoring.** for a mentor, the more willing that protégé is to be vulnerable with that mentor.

The benefit a mentor has is that being a trusted advisor is an expectation of the role. When you are seen as a mentor, you start with a trust deposit with the protégé. Several other factors determine how quickly trust will grow between a mentor and protégé:

- **Interpersonal similarity:** we are more willing to trust those whom we perceive to be like us. When protégés and mentors share characteristics, experiences, beliefs, or values, they are more likely to trust each other. Similarity is not a long-lasting basis of trust, but instead allows initial trust to form more quickly. Other bases of trust take over later.
- **Trust propensity:** some of us are more willing to trust others in general, while others are less willing to trust. This propensity is a

56   *Create a Safe Place*

characteristic of the trustor. If a protégé has a low trust propensity, she will build trust with a mentor less quickly than one with a higher propensity. Like similarity, propensity is more related to how *quickly* trust forms than the *level* of trust (size of the deposit) that will form eventually.

- **Trustworthy actions**: we will trust those who behave in a trustworthy way. There are many elements of trust that are revealed by our actions. Below is a short list of ways to think about how your behavior can build (or erode) a protégé's trust:
  - Reliability: are you someone whose behavior is consistent over time? Do you honor your commitments?
  - Integrity: do your actions match your words?
  - Compassion: do you act in a way that shows you care about the protégé?
  - Competence: does your advice and guidance seem to help the protégé?
- **Interpersonal affect**: we are more willing to trust those with whom we get along well and whom we like. Mentors and protégés who communicate easily and like being around each other will share more trust.
- **Positive results**: over time, trust grows the most when we get good results from mentoring interactions. If, after a meeting with her mentor, a protégé takes action on the discussion and gets a good result, her trust for her mentor will grow. Protégés often start with smaller, lower-risk issues to see if working with a mentor will be beneficial. As the mentoring interaction pays off, trust will grow.

All of these ingredients are considered in making deposits into a protégé's trust account. While a mentor cannot change a protégé's trust propensity, there are many things a mentor can do to build trust more quickly by tapping into the other sources. The sections that follow outline what we have seen mentors do to accelerate trust formation with their protégés.

Getting to Know You

Trust starts by getting to know your protégé. While this point may seem painfully obvious, many mentors do not really know their protégés. They don't know what drives them, what scares them, or what they're really like. A lot of mentors don't get beyond the surface issues their protégés bring. Others delve deeper, but stop at getting to know the professional person. Trust is strongest when you get to know the whole person. It is there that you both find the interpersonal similarity that gets you started, and build the interpersonal affect that is the glue of the relationship.

Early in the mentoring partnership (perhaps the second meeting if you are in a formal program), schedule a meeting devoted to getting to know each other. Send each other your résumés or curricula vitae in advance to get started. To get the most out of the meeting, jot down three to five questions you want to ask your protégé (use the list below to get started). You don't want to make it feel like a formal interview; you just want to have some questions ready so you can have a productive conversation.

Consider having the "get to know you" meeting over a meal. Many of the mentors and protégés with whom I have worked say that sharing a meal together creates a relaxed, comfortable environment to really get to know the other person. Also, think about two or three things about yourself that might be important to share, but your protégé might not think to ask. Remember: this is about letting your protégé get to know you as well.

Getting to Know You Questions

Before your "getting to know you" meeting, select a few questions to get you started. Some protégés open up more easily, so having a few questions ready will help. We covered some basic questions in Chapter 2. Use this longer list to get you thinking.

1. Who have your prior mentors been? What were the most valuable things you learned from them?
2. What's your favorite indoor/outdoor activity?
3. What is your favorite form of exercise?
4. If you could work on only one project for the next year, what would you choose?
5. If you could meet anyone, living or dead, who would you meet?
6. Have you ever had something happen to you that you thought was bad but it turned out to be for the best?
7. What's the hardest thing you've ever done?
8. What is your biggest strength?
9. If you had a long weekend where you could set the agenda, what would you do?
10. What was the first job for which you were paid (and taxes were withheld)? What did you learn from it?
11. If you had it to do over again what would you study in school?
12. What subject do you wish you had paid more attention to in school?
13. What is your dream job?
14. What do you want to do with your retirement?
15. What is the most interesting country you have visited?
16. What do you think about when there is nothing you have to think about?
17. What sports did you play growing up? What musical instrument(s) did you learn growing up?

58 Create a Safe Place

18. If you could go on a vacation anywhere in your country, where would it be?
19. If you could go on a vacation anywhere in the world, where would it be?
20. What is the biggest professional challenge you have overcome?
21. Of what accomplishment are you most proud?
22. What job have you been putting off?
23. What are your most marketable skills?
24. What single piece of technology makes your life easier?
25. What would your ideal party be like? Who would be there?

Meet Frequently (at First)

One thing I've observed over the years working with mentors, as well as through my own mentoring and executive coaching, is that trust takes time to build. Not just calendar time, but meeting time. It takes four to six meetings for trust to build up sufficiently for significant progress to be made. For many mentors in formal mentoring programs that are often designed to last a year, six meetings might not occur until month six or seven, meaning half of the mentoring year is over.

The other benefit of more frequent meetings at first is that you can start to build momentum. If it is four weeks between meetings, a lot of the energy built during the mentoring meeting will dissipate. Use more frequent meetings at the beginning to keep the energy going and use momentum to build trust more quickly. If you meet twice a month for the first three months, you will see more progress sooner.

Make the Meetings a Priority

As noted above, two of the behaviors that communicate that you are trustworthy are reliability and compassion. One of the basic ways you communicate both of these behaviors is how you prioritize meetings with your protégé. Repeatedly canceling and rescheduling meetings makes a protégé feel that your time together is not important. Even being late regularly to meetings sends a message to your protégé. Many protégés are already hesitant to ask for the time of a senior leader they respect. You do not want to reinforce the power distance between the two of you.

While you may have many demands on your time, if you want to build a trusting partnership with your protégé, you need to make mentoring meetings a higher priority than other meetings. If someone else manages your schedule, let him or her know to protect meetings with your protégé as if they were meetings with your boss. If you do have to cancel a meeting, offer to reschedule it. Being available to your protégé is a very basic way to communicate that you are reliable and that you care.

Create a Safe Place 59

Be Fully Present When Meeting

In addition to making the meetings a priority, you want to make sure you are truly present for your protégé during the meeting, which means coming prepared, eliminating distractions, and actively listening to your protégé. Think about meeting with a mentor who checked her phone or let people interrupt your discussion. Not only do the distractions disrupt the flow of the conversation, they remind you that your mentor is not focusing on what you want to discuss, which can erode trust.

You can help your focus by the choice of meeting location. While meeting over a meal can build trust, select a place where you are not going to be around coworkers or others who may interrupt your conversation. Also, switch off your devices to eliminate their ability to distract you. If you are in a situation where you do not feel that you can eliminate all disruptions (for example, there is a crisis at work or at home), you may want to reschedule the meeting. Aside from the possible interruptions, a situation that important may preoccupy your mind and keep you from focusing on the conversation. You should postpone a discussion rather than hold one where you only are devoting part of your attention to your protégé.

Look for Small Wins

Teresa Amabile has written about the power of small wins to motivate. Called the "progress principle," she describes how, in the pursuit of challenging, longer-term goals (the kind that are perfect for mentoring), people can become demotivated by the long slog toward success. Small wins early can help build a protégé's confidence and strengthen the interpersonal affect of the partnership.

What a small win looks like differs by protégé. For one, it might be figuring out how to have a better conversation with a coworker or boss. For another, it might be making a successful presentation to senior leaders. Whatever the win, make sure that you acknowledge it with your protégé. Recognize that it was a hurdle for him and express your excitement in the accomplishment. Climbing the small hills at the beginning of a mentoring partnership makes the big ones you'll encounter later seem more manageable.

Build Your Own Skills

Part of what will build your protégé's trust in you is how effective you are as a mentor. The better your advice, questions, or guidance, the more they will trust you and see you as a mentor. As important as this point is, it is amazing how many mentors underestimate what it takes to be good and do not think about building their own skills. You will have

60 *Create a Safe Place*

an opportunity to build your skills around listening, storytelling, advice giving, and question asking.

When I evaluate mentoring programs, "building my coaching/mentoring skills" is one of the most common benefits mentors report receiving from working with a protégé. Unfortunately, most don't realize how much they are growing until their mentoring partnerships are transitioning. To get the most out of the experience, and to build your skills and trust more quickly, I recommend two basic things the next time you embark on mentoring.

First, set one or two goals related to mentoring or coaching for yourself. They may be as simple as "learn to listen before I talk" or "learn to ask more questions." Setting these goals will get you to focus on improving your skills, and sharing these goals with your protégé will help you seem more accessible.

Second, keep your own learning journal about your mentoring experience. This journal should be different from notes you keep about your mentoring meetings; those notes are likely to be about the **content** of the mentoring conversations, focusing on your protégé's goals. Your mentor's journal should focus on the **process** of mentoring. Keep notes about how much you talked versus listened or how quick you were to offer advice (versus letting your protégé come up with a solution). Writing it down will make it more tangible for you and focus you on improving your skills.

Maintain Confidentiality

If you want to ruin the trust you have built with your protégé, start sharing details of your mentoring conversations with others. For trust to be maintained, your protégé needs to be confident that what you are sharing goes no further than your conversations. If a protégé is truly going to explore difficult issues that are hidden from others, there has to be faith that you can keep them confidential.

There are two challenges with confidentiality. The first involves limits to confidentiality. If you and your protégé work for the same company, and the protégé is aware of illegal or unethical activity and wants to discuss it with you, there may be some fiduciary responsibility that you have as a manager to report it. Your protégé needs to know that going in, and you have to be prepared to handle it if the situation, however unlikely, presents itself.

The second challenge is the protégé's own manager. When it comes to manager quality, it has been my experience that "your mileage may vary." As we saw earlier in the chapter, Pamela was really struggling with her boss, and her mentor, Alana, provided a place for her to vent. Pamela was able to do this because Alana had agreed not to discuss their mentoring conversations with Pamela's boss, even though Alana knew Pamela's boss and had worked with him before. While there may be many reasons you might want to talk about the protégé with his boss (for example, are these the right development goals for the protégé? Are these goals realistic?), they are outweighed by the risks of breaking a protégé's trust, which would cut you and the protégé off from meaningful conversations going forward.

Therefore, there are two rules regarding confidentiality that I recommend: 1. Discuss the limits (if any) to confidentiality with the protégé up front; agree that anything that doesn't approach those limits will be treated as confidential. 2. Agree that you will not discuss your protégé with her or his manager without the protégé's prior permission. Make sure you are explicit about confidentiality. There is a good chance your protégé will begin a discussion with you saying, "Now, this conversation is confidential, right?"

Give (and Seek) Feedback

As you begin to work together, make sure you are giving your protégé feedback on what is and what is not working for you. It is rare for a new relationship to grow without any bumps in the road. Your protégé may check her phone during a meeting, or show up late repeatedly. She may not respond to contact from you in a timely matter, leaving you wondering whether you are going to have to move a meeting time or location. These small issues may start to add up and get in the way of building trust together. You owe it to your protégé to give her feedback on things she is doing that bother you, since she cannot change what she doesn't know.

Keep in mind that, when giving feedback, you are in the more powerful position. While you do not want to sugarcoat your feedback, you also do not want to be so blunt it comes across like a punch in the face. Consider starting your feedback with, "There has been something that has been bothering me a little ..." or "The last few meetings I have been frustrated by ..." Of course, if things have been working well, let your protégé know that as well.

You also want to be overt in asking for feedback, remembering that your protégé may be hesitant or even embarrassed to tell you something you are doing isn't working for her. Open the door with phrases like, "Is there anything I am doing that you would like me to change?" or "If you and I were to make a change to how we are working together, what would it be?" You may have to ask this over the course of several meetings to let the protégé know you would really like to have the feedback. Building regular feedback into your discussions can help keep small issues from growing and can accelerate the trust that you are building together.

62 *Create a Safe Place*

Be Patient

Trust doesn't build overnight. The advice in this chapter can help speed its growth, but you may still face a protégé who is slow to trust. Some have a lower trust propensity, and need more time to trust someone else. Others may not know what are appropriate topics to discuss with a mentor and may not think to venture to the more challenging ones for a while. Still others fear that exposing their vulnerable side will make them appear weak in front of someone senior to them whom they respect.

Whatever the case, you cannot rush trust. It will form at its own speed, and you really cannot force it to go any faster. There may be some protégés with whom you never develop a significant trusting partnership. I have struggled with my own coaching clients who never broke through that wall of trust to really tackle their challenging issues. The best you can do is show patience, make sure you are doing what you can to grow trust, and take whatever trust you and your protégé do build and work with that.

References

Amabile, Teresa M., and Kramer, Steven J. (2011). "The power of small wins." *Harvard Business Review*, 89 (5), 70–80.

Kram, K. (1985). *Mentoring at Work*. Scott, Foresman and Company.

5   Good Questions Beat Good Advice

The wise man doesn't give the right answers, he poses the right questions.
—Claude Levi-Strauss

"This meeting couldn't have come at a better time, Dan. I really need your advice on a situation I am facing." Dan smiled as his protégé, Beverly, sat down. He had really enjoyed the last few months working with her. She had been a program manager for several years and was looking to make the move to director. She spent a lot of their meetings peppering him with questions about what it takes to make the leap from manager to director, always writing down his suggestions and saying, "That is a great idea! I wouldn't have thought of that." Dan looked forward to their meetings because he felt like he was really having an impact.

"What is going on?" Dan asked. Instead of her usual energetic questions, Beverly slumped in her chair a little and sounded exhausted. She explained how two of her project managers were constantly at each others' throats, derailing project update meetings and gossiping to the other project managers about each other. "You should try a team building exercise offsite," Dan began. But, Beverly cut him off, saying she has already tried that. Twice. "Hmmm. Maybe they need a project to work on together. Something that will force them to deal with their issues directly." Beverly had tried that, but it only made the situation worse.

"Well," started Dan as he looked around the conference room for some inspiration, "maybe you could try talking with the two of them separately. I would start with Mike who seems to be the one who ..." but Beverly cut him off. "Look, I've tried that. I'm at the end of my rope. They just hate each other and seem intent on not getting along." Beverly stared at Dan, seemingly waiting for the advice that wasn't coming to him. Dan looked away, frustrated that the advice that seemed to be so helpful to Beverly before was not working.

It occurred to Dan that he had been approaching the situation the wrong way. He looked up at Beverly and said, "It sounds like this situation is a little more complicated than I thought. Can we start over? How long has this been going on?"

64 *Good Questions Beat Good Advice*

"About six months," Beverly replied, looking at the floor between the two of them. "It wasn't like this before. They actually worked pretty well together before that."

Dan perked up. He was suddenly realizing there may be more going on. "What do you think changed?" Beverly furrowed her brow as she considered the question. "Think back," Dan continued. "Did something happen between the two of them? Or, on the team? Tell me about your leadership team about nine months ago."

As Beverly started to talk about the situation, Dan came up with more questions. "What does 'at each others' throats' mean? What are they gossiping about? What did you do for the team building exercise? When you have talked to them individually about the situation, how are you approaching it? What are they saying?" As the questions continued, the story started to unfold, and he and Beverly started to brainstorm new tactics she could take.

Dan's situation is very common. Early in a mentoring partnership, a lot of the discussion is typically about more tactical issues that have tactical solutions. They are issues the mentor has faced before and can be solved with relatively straightforward advice. In fact, the advice helps build the mentor's credibility and the protégé's trust in the mentor. With these early successes, the protégé starts to trust the mentor with more complex issues. That was the situation in which Dan found himself. Beverly saw him as a source of good advice and wanted his thoughts on a situation which was much more complex than what she was raising before. Without realizing it, they had turned the corner from issues where advice would work to an issue where she needed more of a thought partner.

> **Advice is the end of a conversation; a question is the beginning of one.**

Dan had stumbled across the fourth rule of mentoring: Good Questions Beat Good Advice. The advice he gave her on her simpler issues built up her trust in him such that she brought him a much more complex challenge. The advice that had been his primary mentoring tool was no longer working and he needed to try a different tool. More than just being a different approach, questions unlock much of the potential a mentoring partnership can hold. The best mentors do not just dispense advice, they create a conversation that gets a protégé to think. As Dan observed, advice is the end of a conversation; a question is the beginning of one. When your mentoring partnership has turned the corner that Dan and Beverly's did, you will want to shift from dispensing answers to posing questions.

The Power of Questions

Asking questions allows the mentor and protégé to explore the landscape of the protégé's current reality together. Giving advice before adequate

Good Questions Beat Good Advice 65

discovery cuts off this exploration, and fails to honor the simple fact that the protégé knows her or his situation much better than the mentor does. Jump in too early with what you think is good advice and you might miss the mark because it is not a good fit for the situation.

One of the early issues Beverly brought Dan was her struggle to manage her calendar. As a program manager, she was struggling to stay on top of her obligations and found herself working long hours, a situation Dan faced when he was manager several years before. She was inundated with meeting requests from subordinates, peers, and internal customers, and found herself accepting almost all of them even when it was not obvious if she should really be attending. Dan remembered those days and gave her some advice that a former mentor gave him: "No agenda, no attenda." If there is no agenda (and thus no clear purpose for her attending), she should send a rejection back to the meeting organizer that she needs to see the agenda before she can decide whether she should attend. While this may be great advice, a few good questions might uncover the fact that she has never had an administrative assistant dedicated to her and has not taught the assistant to screen the meetings for her, which is what Dan's assistant does for him.

This example brings up another reason questions generally beat advice: your advice may end up treating a symptom and not the root cause. Part of the reason your protégé may be struggling with an issue is because she cannot see beyond the presenting symptom. The issue Beverly faced was less about managing her schedule than managing an assistant. The advice above would have had her continue trying to juggle her own schedule instead of delegating the task and free her up to work on other things. Backing up, Dan could have asked a few different questions to get beyond the presenting problem of having trouble managing her schedule:

- How did your predecessor handle his schedule before you took over?
- How did you deal with meeting requests when you were a supervisor?
- What do your peers do to manage their calendars?

All of these questions prompt the protégé to begin exploring the situation, either by reflecting on the situation with the mentor or by investigating how others are handling similar situations.

Giving advice too early also might start to erode the mentor's credibility, since there is a chance the protégé has already tried what you are suggesting. Every time you suggest something already tried, your protégé loses a little faith that you will be able to help with the current situation. For example, your protégé has a team member who constantly completes assignments at least a day late. Every time the team member has a different, somewhat plausible excuse for why he is late. You ask if he has made sure the team member is reminded of the due date as it approaches. He has. You ask if he has addressed the issue directly with the team member.

66 *Good Questions Beat Good Advice*

He has. You ask if he has talked about the consequences if the situation continues. He has. He is also questioning whether you will be able to help him with the problem.

You can turn around the discussion by asking what your protégé has tried so far. Getting the attempts out on the table does two things. First, it lets the mentor possibly eliminate things that haven't worked yet so your advice can start with new ideas. Second, it gives the mentor a platform for getting the protégé talking about the situation so each option can be explored. An

> I cannot teach anybody anything. I can only make them think.
>
> —Socrates

assumption contained in the discussion above is that not only did the protégé try all of those options, he did all of them well. While he might be reminding the team member of the due date, he might be doing so the day before the assignment is due, which may not be much time for a project that is worked on over the course of a month. Often, exploring these options can uncover a course of action that can be attempted again, but differently, which may yield better results.

Questions also help keep the ownership of the problems as well as their solutions with the protégé, a point that was emphasized in the first rule, Lead by Following. Many mentors are tempted by their protégé's problems because many mentors love solving problems. They often have achieved their positions within their organizations by being able to solve problems. This strength can turn into a liability if they get drawn into a trap of solving problems for their protégés. Instead of having a thought partner who challenges them to think, the protégé is taught to bring challenges to the mentor, sometimes even establishing a pattern of dependence on the mentor. The protégé is robbed of the opportunity to learn to solve their issues themselves and build their own confidence.

In addition to curtailing his learning, the protégé is also executing someone else's idea instead of his own. The protégé does not own the solution. You can tell the difference between someone who is following a course of action they came up with and trying something a mentor suggested. The ownership makes a big difference in how a protégé approaches a challenge.

Finally, questions can be powerful relationship builders between a mentor and protégé. Engaging in an exploratory conversation can help the partners get to know one another better and deepen the trust they have built. Handing out advice is very transactional, and it reinforces to the protégé the power differential between you and him or her. A series of exploratory questions allows you to understand the protégé's world better and drive more challenging thinking that will often grow the protégé's capabilities.

Is There a Role for Advice?

Why then, you might ask, do so many mentors think their primary role is to give advice? It is not that giving advice plays no role in mentoring; in fact, a lot of mentoring relationships begin with advice. Protégés seek mentors because they are seeking solutions. The quickest way to a solution is giving advice. Asking questions can be a long, drawn-out process of inquiry and introspection. Questions require patience and trust. Early in a mentoring partnership, the trust required to have a robust dialogue may not have been established yet. Furthermore, solving a problem is rewarding to the mentor. If a protégé brings you a problem and you are able to give a solution, you feel good. You also feel smart and capable.

As a result, a dynamic gets set up between the mentor and protégé: the protégé gets an answer to her or his question, and the mentor feels good about being able to help someone else. Unfortunately, this self-reinforcing dynamic becomes a trap (as seen at the beginning of the chapter) from which it can be difficult to escape. Dispensing advice is only the first, and easiest, level of mentoring. If a mentor and protégé remain in the problem–advice dynamic, they miss much of the power that comes from mentoring. The first step in managing the advice vs. questions dichotomy is to recognize what sort of issue your protégé has brought you.

Anatomy of Issues

There is a seemingly infinite list of topics protégés want to discuss with their mentors. They can range from "How do I manage my calendar better?" or "How can I grow my network?" all the way through to "How do I repair the culture of my startup company after I had to fire an executive who was wrecking it?" While the list of issues can feel overwhelming, many of them possess a basic anatomy that gives you a clue for how to approach them.

There are some issues for which advice giving is very appropriate. These issues tend to be less complex and have not caused the protégé much anguish (yet). As the trust grows between you and your protégé and you are able to help with these less complex challenges, your protégé will see you as a credible source for help and will begin to bring more complex issues into the conversation. It is this complexity that shows growth in trust in a mentoring partnership. Therefore, the first sign of the issue's anatomy is its complexity. As you saw with Dan and Beverly, protégé issues can jump in complexity with little warning.

The other basic factor in the anatomy is the amount of emotional load for the protégé. There are some issues that have a strong emotional component that complicates the issue itself. The protégé may be experiencing fear, doubt, anger, or frustration with the issue. The stronger these emotions, the harder it is for a protégé to approach the situation. The emotions create a cloud around the issue, making it hard to think about.

68 *Good Questions Beat Good Advice*

This emotional component must be dealt with for the protégé to be able to talk about the issue. When you combine complexity with emotional load, you get an anatomy of three types of protégé issues. We'll call them Hands, Head, and Heart issues.

Hands: These issues are less complex and carry with them little emotional charge. These issues don't require a lot of trust to talk about, and are usually knowledge gaps that usually close over time with experience. Mentors can often use advice for these issues to help a protégé find a course of action. Examples of hands issues include:

- Time management
- Building a network
- Meeting management
- Short-term goal setting and planning
- Project management.

Head: These issues are more complex and may start to have some emotional charge to them. Protégés usually have some experience with the issue and are in need of some perspective or distance. The protégé may have the answer, but hasn't put it together yet, or needs confirmation that it is the right answer. Mentors use questions for these issues to get a protégé to take a different perspective and consider the challenge in a different way. Typical head issues you might encounter include:

- Coaching a difficult employee
- Using influence without authority
- Leading change
- Dealing with conflict
- Creating longer-term plans (e.g., career strategy or project plans).

Heart: These issues can be the most complex, and usually evoke strong emotions with the protégé. The issue could be something causing the protégé stress now, or a topic that the protégé is avoiding because of the stress involved with thinking about it. The protégé may be experiencing some inner conflict about it that is fueling strong emotions. It is these issues where a mentor's empathy plays a key role. Common heart issues you may come across include:

- Working with a demanding or difficult boss
- Dealing with peers who have agendas
- Questioning long-held assumptions (especially separating "how it should be" from "how it is")
- Facing significant fears (e.g., public speaking)
- Coping with prolonged conflict
- Recovering from failures, especially when aspirations are not met.

Good Questions Beat Good Advice   69

Let's examine the same issue existing at the three different levels. For this example, each protégé is working in the marketing organization of a manufacturing company. The issue is exploring career opportunities in a different division within marketing.

Hands: Manuel is an associate in the commercial products division and wants to explore a move to the consumer products division. He is junior in the organization and doesn't really know anyone in the other division. His mentor suggests conducting some informational interviews in consumer products and helps Manuel get a few meetings to get started.

Head: Theresa is a supervisor in the commercial products division who isn't enjoying her work in her division. The company is investing more in the consumer products side, and she wants to work on those projects. Because she doesn't have much experience on that side of marketing, she would, at best, make a lateral move if not take a step back career wise. In the meantime, she is being considered for a manager's job in commercial products, which would be a significant step ahead. For Theresa, she needs to explore her options and think through what she really wants. Her mentor uses questions to help her think through what course of action would make the most long-term sense for her.

Heart: Andreas is a manager in the commercial products division who feels like his career is stalling. He sees the consumer products side grow with the company's investments, and feels like he would be better off long term working there. The marketing director of a major consumer product line has been talking to him about coming to work for her, but the situation isn't that simple. She and Andreas's current boss have a very bad relationship, and are often on opposite sides of company politics. Andreas is struggling with issues of loyalty to his current boss and fears becoming a political football between the two of them.

Moving from hands to head to heart issues reflects growth in trust between a mentor and protégé. We will tackle heart issues more in the next chapter. For now, we will focus on transitioning from hands to head issues.

Asking Questions

Asking questions as a mentor is a skill to be honed and practiced. The first thing to remember from the mentoring rule Lead by Following is that a question like, "Have you tried talking with your boss about that?" is not actually a question. It is advice masquerading as a question. You are telling your protégé, "I think you ought to talk to your boss about that." While that is a legitimate question to ask, especially when you and your protégé are testing out different ideas, it really isn't a question as described here. The goal of asking questions is to get the protégé to solve

70   *Good Questions Beat Good Advice*

the problem and choose a course of action him or herself. Feeding your protégé an answer, while helpful, doesn't build this capacity. There are two basic classes of questions that promote protégé thinking: Exploratory and Insight.

Exploratory Questions

Exploratory questions seek information to understand the situation. Listen in on the exchange below between a mentor and her protégé:

WEI (PROTÉGÉ): So, I feel like I'm getting conflicting information from my direct boss and my dotted line boss.

BARB (MENTOR): What did your direct boss ask you to do?

WEI: He wanted me to relocate my team to be in closer proximity to his other direct reports so I can "integrate better" with them, whatever that means.

BARB: What did your dotted line boss want you to do?

WEI: She thinks my team should stay where we are now, which is closer to the other portfolio teams. She thinks there is more business benefit to the synergy that comes from portfolio integration instead of product line integration.

BARB: What do your peers think? The ones on the product side?

WEI: They don't think my team is integrating as well as we should …

These questions are relatively straightforward and have as their primary purpose to explore the situation. They attempt to answer Who, What, When, Where, and How types of questions. In the scenario, Barb is getting the lay of the land with Wei, trying to understand what he is facing, who the players are, etc. At this point, the mentor isn't trying to take the protégé anywhere; Barb is just setting the scene so she can understand the situation better. Remember: your protégé always understands her or his situation better than you do.

Basic exploratory questions help you establish:

- Who is involved in the situation?
- What is each party's interest?
- What is the primary challenge?
- What constraints does the protégé face?
- What time constraints are at work?

As you ask the exploratory questions, you are helping your protégé reexamine the situation with some distance and some perspective. Sometimes, when your protégé hears herself describing the situation, she comes to a resolution and course of action on her own. While it may not feel as satisfying as giving advice that makes your protégé light up, you are actually

Good Questions Beat Good Advice 71

helping your protégé grow. Beyond that, you are teaching your protégé to start using you as a sounding board, which is another powerful role of a mentor.

Insight Questions

Insight questions are different, in that they push the protégé to think. You are trying to get the protégé to take other perspectives, put together disparate information, or face uncomfortable truths. When we are facing complicated situations, we tend to narrow our thinking or be blind to alternatives. In asking questions, you are trying to expand your protégé's thinking and start to see more possibilities. For example, after the initial exchange above, Barb might have asked the following questions of Wei:

- What do you believe is motivating your direct manager's wish for you to relocate your team? What do you think is behind your dotted line boss's resistance?
- Of the choices facing you, which makes more sense to you? For the business?
- If you make a change, how will that affect those around you?

All of these questions are designed to get the protégé to change the lenses through which he or she is looking at the issue. They ask the protégé to think more deeply about the situation and go beyond the surface of the issues being put forward. The insight question is designed to engage the brain and spark some additional thinking about the situation. Your goal is to promote thinking beyond the protégé's initial understanding of the situation and delve into the complexities of what the situation holds. Insight questions come in many varieties, including the following:

- Logical: What could have caused that to happen?
- Enabling: You have mentioned that as a barrier; what could you do to start climbing over or working around that barrier?
- Comparison: How have others handed similar situations?
- Contrasting: How is this situation different than ones you have experienced before?
- Visionary: What does success look like for you?

Insight questions are primarily used to take a protégé to another level of understanding of her or his situation and fully explore the head issue. There are times when they are used to challenge a protégé. You may need to challenge assumptions a protégé has about a situation, or challenge him to go beyond what he has done in the past. Challenge questions

72   *Good Questions Beat Good Advice*

are powerful, but run the risk of triggering defensiveness. They rely on a fair amount of trust to have been built between mentor and protégé and must be asked in a way that does not feel threatening to a protégé. Keep in mind the third rule of mentoring, Create a Safe Place. Below are some ways to ask challenging questions in ways that make the protégé feel safe:

Situation	Possibly Threatening	Safer
Your protégé seems frustrated that his boss won't make time to talk about his development.	Why don't you just ask her to talk about it?	What would happen if you asked her during your next meeting?
Your protégé has been a director for six months and wants to get promoted to VP in a year.	No one gets promoted here that quickly. Why do you think you can get it done so fast?	That seems like an ambitious schedule. Who else would be considered for that position? How do you compare to them?
Your protégé knows that she needs to network more to take more control of her career. She proposes having one lunch meeting a month with senior leaders.	I don't think that will be enough. Why don't you set a goal of four a month?	What is your thinking behind one meeting a month? That is twelve meetings a year; how many contacts will you need to grow your network? Is there another reason you're choosing one a month?

You may notice that in each of the safer questions above, the mentor avoided using the word "why." It is a subtle semantic issue, but the word "why" often puts a protégé back on his heels, forcing him into a defensive stance. Even asking, "Why do you think your boss won't devote time to your development?" puts your protégé in the position of having to defend his boss's behavior. If you can, avoid asking "why" and turn them into "what" questions.

Why?	What?
Why would your boss do that?	What could be your boss's reasons for her decision?
It seems like it might help your career. Why don't you want to take on that project?	That project seems like it would help you further your goals. What is your hesitation about it?
Do your peers struggle with this issue? Why do you think it gives you problems?	Is this issue common among your peers? What is different about your situation?

Good Questions Beat Good Advice 73

To be truly effective at insight questions, you must remind yourself that you are not trying to solve the head issue yourself, but trying to solve it *with* your protégé. As you start asking these types of questions you need to keep in mind that you are probably working down some logical question chain that makes sense to you. Don't forget to invite your protégé into the problem-solving process. Make sure you set up your questions with some context and help him understand why you are asking the questions you are.

A simple acronym, SARA, might help you when you are asking insight questions:

1. Set Up the Question. When you and your protégé are working through an issue together, both of your brains are engaged separately. You are evaluating information your protégé shares, looking for connections and meaning, and formulating new ideas. Sometimes, the question you want to ask is the result of a chain of three or four ideas that were in your brain. Before throwing out a question that seems like it is coming out of the blue, set it up with your train of thoughts. Share your thinking that led you to the question so your protégé understands how you arrived at it.
2. Ask the Question. Pose the question you want to ask and avoid starting with the word "why" if you can. Then, be quiet. Let your protégé consider the question. Let her think about it for a little while. If you are truly trying to promote insight, she may need a little time to consider an answer. If you get impatient with silence, slowly count to ten in your head. You do not want to jump in too quickly and take over the discussion.
3. Reflect the Answer. Paraphrase the answer you heard before going too much further. Sometimes, the first answer the protégé gives hasn't been thought through, and she needs to hear it back to think about it more. Reflecting also checks to make sure you understood the answer so that the next step you take is in the same direction as the protégé is going. Finally, paraphrasing keeps the ball in the protégé's court for a little longer. It may spur other ideas that occur to her upon hearing back her own words. Keep in mind that you want to Lead by Following. If you can keep the problem solving with the protégé, you are empowering her to think.
4. Ask or Act. The next step is to ask the next question (e.g., What would happen if you tried that?) or to move the protégé toward some action (e.g., When do you think you could give that a try?). If there is more to the issue the protégé needs to consider, keep the questions and dialogue going. If the protégé seems to be arriving at a set of actions he can take as a result, start exploring the next steps.

Dealing with head issues is when mentoring can be most powerful for a protégé. You are helping to build capabilities and confidence at the same

74 *Good Questions Beat Good Advice*

time. While the feedback is not as immediate as the good feeling you get watching a protégé write down a piece of advice you just gave her, the payoff for the protégé is multiplied many times over.

Belief and Desire

There are times when asking questions feels like spinning your wheels. You throw out questions, but they don't seem to spark any new thinking. Instead, your protégé focuses on reasons why ideas won't work. You try approaching the issue from different angles, but your protégé keeps coming back to the same reasons and nothing he can do will change the situation. There is something missing for the protégé that no amount of insight questions will solve.

Garrett was in sales for a software company that sold applications to hospitals. He was on an account for a hospital that was the worst customer he ever encountered. The IT staff at the hospital were very demanding, soaking up a lot of his time and that of the software developers in his company. He was sure that they were losing money servicing the account, and he was personally sacrificing a lot of his time to keep them happy. He kept telling his boss that they needed to change how they were dealing with the hospital or drop them as a customer. His boss told him the hospital was too important to gaining new business. They had won a lot of business by pointing to that hospital as a customer.

That answer didn't make Garrett feel much better, and he spent a lot of his time with his mentor, Rashid, talking about how he could make his case better to his boss that they needed to change the relationship with the hospital. In the middle of another meeting discussing the customer, Rashid leaned back in his chair and asked, "Let me ask you this, Garrett. Do you think you can change this situation at all?" Stunned, Garrett paused a second, then said, "I don't know. That's part of the problem."

All of us need two ingredients to take a productive approach to the problems we face. We must **believe** that we can have some impact on the situation, and we have to **desire** the change enough to do something about it. Furthermore, these two elements interact like a multiplication equation: if either value is zero, the whole answer is zero. If the protégé doesn't believe he can affect the situation in a positive way, any action taken is likely to be half-hearted or incomplete. No matter how much he wants his situation to change, he won't be able to change it unless he believes he can. Conversely, if he lacks the desire to do what it will take to change the situation, no amount of belief is going to spur him to action.

Rashid realized that Garrett couldn't see a way out of his situation and was stuck in his belief that there was nothing he could do. No amount of questions Rashid could ask about solving the problem would yield a productive path forward without that belief. Even if Rashid were able to

Good Questions Beat Good Advice 75

get Garrett to follow some of his advice for the situation, actions Garrett would take would be hampered by an internal doubt in their efficacy. The best course of action for the mentor would be to address the belief and desire directly.

Belief

With respect to belief, there are two avenues you can pursue as a mentor. First, you can try to restore belief with the protégé that he can have a positive impact on his situation. You can ask what forces are preventing change and sustaining the status quo. Explore those forces with the protégé. Is he overestimating their power or importance? Is Garrett's boss that firm about the current approach to the hospital? Could she be persuaded to try an alternative? Is there a bigger picture the protégé is missing? For instance, is Garrett's boss changing the dynamics with the customer, just more slowly than Garrett would like? You may be able to chip away at the forces that are keeping the protégé from moving forward.

Another tactic to try is to look for examples of when the protégé has been successful changing similar situations. Has Garrett been able to persuade the boss on other issues? If so, what made him successful in those instances? Have others been able to persuade the boss? If your protégé cannot point to his own examples, do you have any to share? You may be able to help the protégé see his own situation differently by comparing it to your example. Finally, if your protégé is not breaking through his own belief barrier, you may want to express your own belief in your protégé and ask him to trust in that belief. This final tactic requires a fair amount of trust and is a risk to the trust the two of you have built.

On the other hand, your protégé may be in a situation where the forces supporting the status quo truly are too difficult to surmount. While it may be difficult to give up on the issue, you may have to redirect the protégé to other topics. If this were the case with Garrett, Rashid might say, "I know this issue is important to you, but it doesn't seem like you can find a path forward. I am happy to keep talking about it if you need a place to vent, but I'm wondering if there are other issues you and I can tackle where we would have more success?" While you do not want to cut off your support for a difficult situation (see the next rule, Balance Empathy and Action), you may want to move your protégé on to challenges that he believes he can change.

Desire

The second half of the equation can be trickier because it has more emotion at its core. The desire to take action would seem to be a given; otherwise, your protégé wouldn't be bringing up the issue. But, there may

76 *Good Questions Beat Good Advice*

be something that is holding the protégé back. She may truly believe that she can change the situation, but she is not taking action because she is the one who is holding back the change. As journalist Sydney J. Harris said, "Our dilemma is that we hate change and love it at the same time; what we really want is for things to remain the same but get better."

Three basic reasons your protégé may lack the desire to change are failing in the past, learning to live with it, and fearing the change. Your protégé may have already tried to change the situation before, but the change has failed to take hold or to last. The failure could be that she tried the wrong tactics or executed them the wrong way. "I've tried to talk to my boss about that, but she doesn't listen," she may say. She may believe that the situation can change, but has lost the desire to continue to try to change it. You can address past failure by asking questions about the tactic itself: "Do you need to bring your boss evidence from customers to change her mind? Is just bringing it up going to convince her?" You may also ask how the tactic was executed: "When you talked to your boss, what did it sound like?" You may uncover that the protégé is hinting at the problem or complaining loudly about it instead of engaging in a true dialogue with her boss. You may be able to rekindle desire by helping the protégé find tactics that will be more effective.

Of course, it may be that the protégé has found the right solution and is doing it the right way, but she has not been consistent in its application. Think of the times you have been motivated to change something about yourself and have gotten off to a great start. You start going to the gym, staying off of caffeine, or changing your diet. You have a great few weeks, but then you slip into your old habits and the change fails to take hold. The next time you want to make the change again, you remember your past failure and lose some of the enthusiasm and energy needed to make the change. We will explore how a mentor can help a protégé here in an upcoming rule, Foster Accountability.

It may also be that your protégé has learned to live with the situation. While it is not the solution she wants, she has found some equilibrium with the current level of discomfort. It may be that the pain comes in small doses (the protégé is able to avoid the situation most days), or the pain comes sharply and then fades for a while. These situations can be insidious, since they wear a protégé down over time. The toll they exact is death by a thousand cuts. This situation is more difficult to attack directly since the protégé has found some measure of peace with it for now. You can bring the issue up from time to time to check, but you may be better off redirecting the protégé to other topics and only revisit it during times when the desire seems to have returned.

Finally, your protégé's desire to change can be negated by her fear of actually changing. She may fear damaging relationships (If I speak up, will my boss not like me?), fear failing (If it doesn't work, will my boss

Good Questions Beat Good Advice 77

trust me?), or fear making things worse (If I bring it up, will others think I am a complainer?). Fear is the greatest enemy of desire and can keep your protégé from addressing situations that she can change for the better. Helping a protégé cope with fear (and other emotions) will be covered in the next rule, Balance Empathy and Action.

If your protégé can restore both belief and desire to take action, the two of you can return to asking questions to help your protégé come up with new solutions to try. In fact, helping a protégé cope with belief and desire can strengthen your partnership further.

Giving Advice

Just because asking questions tends to be more powerful in moving a protégé than giving advice, there are times when advice can play an important role in mentoring. First, at the start of a mentoring partnership, advice is often seen as the currency of mentoring. That is, a protégé evaluates whether she or he will want to work with a mentor based on the quality of advice that is shared. Advice often is used at the beginning of a mentoring relationship to establish that initial credibility that forms the basis of trust.

Advice can also play an important role for hands issues when there is a short list of potential solutions the protégé might try. The advice is used to close these knowledge gaps. For instance, Colleen's protégé feels he is getting pigeon-holed in the sales organization and wants to grow his professional network into marketing. She suggests setting up an informational interview with a manager in marketing and joining one of three different associations for marketing professionals. Her advice jump-started her protégé's activity toward his goal, as he didn't really know how to get started.

Finally, advice is useful when the protégé has a good grip on the situation, but cannot see what to do next. As you know, when you are facing a stressful challenge, the answer is often sitting right in front of you; you just need to have someone point it out. In these cases, even if the advice isn't the obvious thing to do, it can often reengage a protégé who had started to give up. The advice might be treated as the start of a brainstorming process that leads to an eventual solution.

When you are in one of these situations, giving advice can be your ally, if you do it right. Below are some thoughts to consider when giving advice:

- Start with questions. Make sure you understand the situation and find out what the protégé has already tried.
- Present the advice without being forceful. If you lead with, "You ought to do this," the mentor still owns the solution. Presenting

78 *Good Questions Beat Good Advice*

it with a question, "Have you tried this?" or "Do you think this might work?" or less forcefully, "You might consider trying this," allows the protégé to reject it if it doesn't feel like a good fit. Or, it might spur your protégé to start thinking again and taking more ownership.

- Use it to start brainstorming. "Let's call that Option 1. What other ideas do you think we can come up with?"

The next chapter will explore this notion more fully, examining the role of showing empathy as issues become more complex and are often saturated with emotions.

6   Balance Empathy and Action

Eric's voice was shaky as he retold the story to Amanda, his mentor. He told her about the meeting two days ago with his boss, who informed him about the change in the project. About how Paul was going to be leading it. Paul, the kiss-up, who spent more time schmoozing with the managers than doing his job. Paul, whom Eric had to bail out on numerous occasions. Eric's boss said that the request for Paul came from the director and that he couldn't change his mind. Eric's boss still wanted him on the project because he knows Eric will bail Paul out when the project runs into troubles. Not "if"; "when." How could they give the project to Paul?!

Amanda sat back and surveyed Eric. His eyes were flashing, his fists clenched on the conference room table. His breathing was quick and shallow, and his face had become a bright red. She sat forward, eying Eric, and said, "Well, what are you going to do about it?"

All of the energy seemed to drain from Eric's body as he slumped in the chair. "I don't know. I do everything right. I do what's right for the company, everything they ask of me. This is how they repay me."

"That kind of talk isn't going to get you anywhere," Amanda quipped. "Unless you are ready to do something about it, nothing will change. What can you do to change things?"

Eric sank a little lower in his chair. He could feel the fury quickly draining from his veins. His fists unclenched and became cold. He stared blankly at the spot on the table between him and Amanda. "I don't know."

The meeting didn't last long after that. Amanda left frustrated with Eric's lack of action. Eric felt drained, like he lost the only ally he thought he had. Without realizing it, Amanda was breaking the fifth rule of mentoring: Balance Empathy and Action.

Amanda and Eric's experience is familiar to many mentoring pairs. As the trust between a mentor and protégé grows, the protégé starts to bring more emotionally charged, heart issues into the conversation. Such conversations are markers of a higher level of trust being developed. How a mentor handles these conversations will have an impact on what action the protégé takes, as well as the development of the overall mentoring relationship. On the surface, it would appear that

80   *Balance Empathy and Action*

Eric is coming to Amanda with a problem that he wants to solve. She sees it as a head issue, one that needs to be explored and discussed rationally to find a solution. Because she was responding to the issue at its surface (what should Eric do), Amanda went straight into problem solving and didn't address the emotional load that Eric was carrying. While Eric may have wanted to explore options about his situation, that wasn't what he was seeking at the outset even if he couldn't articulate it. For him, his situation was a heart issue, one that carried with it an emotional burden that needed to be addressed before he could get to the head component of the problem. In the end, he was looking for someone to empathize with him.

Empathy in Mentoring

Believing that someone else can connect with how you are feeling is very powerful as it taps into many fundamental emotional needs we all share. At a basic level, we all want to feel **understood**, like someone else "gets" us. When a mentor connects by empathizing, we feel like someone understands us. Beyond the basic connection, we also want to feel like we are **not alone** in facing a challenge. We are looking for an ally who will take our side or, at least, acknowledge our feelings about the situation. A mentor can be a natural ally that helps us feel like someone is in our corner, someone who can help us figure things out and decide on a course of action.

While Eric would probably benefit from connecting with Amanda, his situation reinforces other roles empathy plays. Eric is a strong performer who has always been able to work hard and get recognized for it. He has built a worldview that has a very basic equation built into it: Good work leads to good things. Since Paul has come onto the scene, Paul is disrupting that equation. In Eric's mind, Paul does not do good work. Yet, Paul still gets recognition and rewards, in this case being elevated by the director. How Paul operates has been bothering Eric for a while, piling up the frustration with Eric's perceived injustice.

This may be the first time Eric has had to face a situation where his great work didn't speak for itself, and where he was watching a peer who wasn't working as hard get more recognition. Not only does he feel alone, he feels like he is **the only one** who has faced this situation. To an outsider, Eric's thoughts may seem irrational; he himself may be unaware of what, exactly, he feels about the situation. But, when you are Eric, facing a situation you don't know how to solve that runs counter to your core beliefs, you may be looking for someone else to say, "I've been in your shoes." That validation, that someone else has faced the same thing, helps you let go of some of the frustration; this person is confirming that others have faced this situation before and that there may be a solution.

Balance Empathy and Action 81

After the sense of relief that comes from someone being able to understand my situation and truly empathize, a mentor can also **validate** that it's okay for the protégé to feel this way. While Eric's feelings may not be entirely rational (feelings rarely are, which is why they are feelings and not reason), they are real for Eric. Unless a mentor takes the time to empathize with a protégé, the emotions will continue to get in the way, keeping the protégé from seeing a way out of the situation.

Sympathy vs. Empathy

Many mentors confuse empathy and sympathy. The conflation of the two is easy to understand, as both serve to acknowledge that the protégé is in a situation that he or she finds less than desirable and are offered as a way to show support. However, sympathy has a different effect on the protégé and on the relationship with the mentor.

If you look up the definitions of the two terms, you will find that to empathize is to _understand and share the feelings of another_, whereas to sympathize is to _feel pity or sorrow for another's situation_. The former is about a shared experience, a connection the protégé has with the mentor. The latter is an offering of condolence for the protégé's circumstance, but not a sharing of the experience. When a protégé is bringing an emotional issue to a mentor, he is not looking for pity; he is looking for someone to say, "I've been there, and I've felt what you are feeling."

Showing sympathy has the potential to create _more_ distance with the protégé, making the protégé feel even more alone, as if he is the only one who has experienced this issue before. That is not to say that sympathy would be unwelcome from a mentor; the protégé may not feel he has anywhere else to bring this issue and have someone acknowledge his predicament. But, being able to truly empathize with the protégé has the potential to create a stronger bond between mentor and protégé and initiate a conversation where the protégé can explore his situation from the perspective of someone who has been there.

Emotion-Feedback Cycle

As you saw in the last chapter, emotions can be an important part of the issues a protégé will face. These are generally heart issues, ones that bring an emotional burden to their complexity. Heart issues can be particularly thorny, because they are part of the emotion-feedback cycle. Showing empathy helps break the emotion-feedback cycle we experience when our stress levels are going up.

The cycle is that relationship between the rational and the emotional sides of our brain. When a situation has an emotional charge to it, our emotion center kicks in and starts to become more vigilant, attending to the stimuli around us. But, it doesn't just take in the stimuli; it changes

82 *Balance Empathy and Action*

how we perceive the stimuli, and even what stimuli we pay attention to. Psychologists call this confirmation bias. We tend to pay more attention to and give more weight to evidence that supports our beliefs and emotions, while discounting or rationalizing evidence that contradicts what we already think or feel.

An example may help shed light on the situation. In the beginning of the chapter, we met Eric and learned about the frustration he was having with his coworker, Paul. As you may guess, Eric is laboring under the assumption that hard work will be rewarded, and that the bosses will see through what Eric considers Paul's sycophantic schmoozing. Whenever he deals with Paul, Eric's stress levels go up. Eric doesn't have a lot of professional respect for Paul; the success Paul enjoys frustrates Eric, since it flies in the face of one of Eric's core beliefs.

Unfortunately, Eric's emotional reaction to Paul colors his rational assessment of Paul. If you were to ask Eric, he would describe Paul as technically inept, lazy, and a kiss-up. However, if you were to ask a peer who doesn't have the same attitude toward Paul, she might describe Paul as competent technically (not a star, but certainly capable enough) but a great people person. Paul is friendly and easy to talk to, part of what makes him a great networker.

Two people observe the same person through different lenses. Unfortunately, Eric's lens causes him to look for evidence that supports his idea of Paul and ignore other evidence. It also causes him to observe the same behavior differently. When others observe Paul networking with those above him, Eric sees someone sucking up and acting political. This feedback cycle can be very difficult to break. We often hold on to our beliefs and assumptions, especially when they elicit a strong emotional reaction. In fact, the stronger the emotions, the more impervious the beliefs are to logical examination. What would be, on its surface, a head issue that needs a logical solution has wound itself up into a heart issue. Only by acknowledging and addressing the emotional component can the protégé begin to let go of the emotions and change lenses.

Steps to Empathy

To help break the emotion-feedback cycle, mentors will need to address the emotional component of the heart issues. A first step is to consider what emotions the protégé is experiencing. This seemingly simple first step is key, because naming the feeling often helps the protégé lessen the grip it has on him. Figuring out what emotions are being felt is far from easy, as the more challenging heart issues often carry with them several emotions that the protégé may not be able to easily articulate. Building your emotional vocabulary is a good place to start, as it will help you better understand what is causing your protégé difficulty.

Give the Feelings a Name

One way to help unravel the grip emotions have on your protégé is to name the feeling. Acknowledging the feeling by naming it helps the protégé feel that you understand him and opens up the dialogue to explore the feeling and the effect it is having on him. Emotions can be complex, and several emotions can be at work with one situation. Start by listening to your protégé talk about the situation and try to identify what feeling is at work.

Below is a list of the emotions that we experience when facing difficult situations. Use the list below to familiarize yourself with more emotion words. Recognize that many words that seem synonymous at first reflect subtle differences in feeling states. For instance, you can see that *leery* is different than *cautious*, and *resentful* is not the same as *bitter*.

Afraid	Embarrassed	Jealous
Agitated	Encouraged	Jittery
Angry	Enraged	Joyous
Anxious	Enthused	Leery
Apprehensive	Exasperated	Lonely
Ashamed	Excited	Miserable
Awkward	Exhausted	Moody
Bewildered	Fatigued	Nervous
Bitter	Fearful	Numb
Brave	Fidgety	Overwhelmed
Calm	Frightened	Pessimistic
Cautious	Frustrated	Pleased
Cheerful	Furious	Proud
Comfortable	Grateful	Puzzled
Concerned	Gloomy	Regretful
Confident	Grouchy	Rejected
Confused	Guilty	Reluctant
Content	Happy	Resentful
Curious	Hassled	Restless
Cynical	Helpless	Rushed
Depressed	Hesitant	Sad
Delighted	Hopeful	Safe
Disappointed	Hostile	Scared
Discouraged	Hurt	Secure
Disgusted	Impatient	Shocked
Distressed	Inferior	Shy
Down	Insecure	Sorry
Eager	Irate	Stressed
Edgy	Irritated	Surprised

84   *Balance Empathy and Action*

Suspicious	Troubled	Weary
Terrified	Unsettled	Wonderful
Tired	Upset	Worried
Torn		

Notice that some of the words are positive, which reveals some of the complexity of emotion. Not only do protégés experience multiple emotions at the same time about a single issue, they may also experience conflicting emotions. Imagine how a software engineer might feel if he were offered a promotion to supervisor where he would be responsible for the work of five other engineers. He might feel *proud* that management thought enough of him to ask. He might also feel *frustrated* that several of his peers were promoted before he was. He also may feel *apprehensive* of the additional responsibility that comes with managing others. Finally, he may have a (perhaps false) level of *confidence* that he can do the job. All of these feelings get wrapped together and make the decision difficult to process. Having a mentor to unravel these emotions can lessen the hold they have and make it easier for the protégé to make a decision.

Ask Feeling Questions

Many times, protégés don't offer up their feelings very readily. Even if you have a well-developed emotional lexicon, the emotions that are gripping your protégé may need some work to unpack and understand. It helps to develop your skills in asking about emotions and getting comfortable having the feelings conversation. Asking feeling questions is usually not difficult. You can start with the easy question, "How does that make you feel?" It may sound trite or clichéd, but that question can often get a protégé started. It suggests that you are open to having the feeling conversation as well as confirming that it is okay for the protégé to feel something about the situation.

The response your protégé gives may be the most salient emotion he is feeling. Before you start to explore the first emotion, you may want to ask, "That makes sense. What else does it make you feel?" Often, emotions travel in packs, and more than one needs to be given a voice. It may be that the protégé shares the "easy" emotion, the one that may be more obvious or least threatening. It may take some trust to get to the other emotions, which could take a little work and patience.

At the beginning of the chapter, we saw Eric grappling with his emotions about his situation with his colleague Paul. Instead of jumping right into action, Amanda, the mentor, could have asked him a little about how the situation made him feel. Right off the bat, he may have said that

Balance Empathy and Action 85

he feels angry or frustrated. While valid, those emotions probably only scratch the surface, and likely reflect how it is making Eric feel *right now*. They are likely symptoms of deeper feelings that are causing this situation to be difficult for him.

A little more digging would reveal that Eric is feeling confused. He doesn't understand why his hard work isn't being recognized. He may also feel helpless, that he doesn't know what to do about the situation. These emotions get to a deeper level of why the situation is causing Eric strife. They get closer to the root of the issue, which may be Eric's belief that all he needs to do is work hard to get recognized. Exploring these feelings would help Eric and Amanda get to the root of the issue. If, instead, they jumped over these feelings and started talking about what action Eric could take, they would have likely missed the opportunity to explore his feelings and get to the root cause.

Sometimes, the "How does that make you feel?" question elicits an "I don't know" response. For some protégés, talking about feelings is a risky conversation. Many of us don't like to admit that we have an emotional side that affects us or how we see the world. For many protégés, admitting that they are affected by their feelings means that they have lost some measure of control. As a mentor, you may have to open the door for your protégé and admit that you have had similar feelings as well. Doing so makes you vulnerable, but is a great demonstration of trust and empathy. If your protégé is struggling to name his or her feelings, you might ask this question: "If I were in your shoes, I might feel _____. Is that how you feel?" The emotion you name might not be the one the protégé is feeling, but it can be the start of the conversation. If that isn't the emotion, you can follow up with, "If that isn't it, what do you think you are feeling?"

Feel the Protégé's Emotional State

After you are able to name some of the complex emotions your protégé is facing, it helps to see if you can personally connect to her state of mind. Remember: more power comes from empathy than sympathy. Use the exercise below to get started.

Take a moment to reflect on strong emotions that you have felt in the past. Think of an emotion-laden situation you have faced in the last six to nine months. It could be a struggle at work that caused anger, fear, or frustration. It could be a family situation that was causing anxiety or stress. It could be a health issue with which a loved one was coping. It doesn't have to be the same situation your protégé is facing; it just has to carry a similar emotional load. Write notes about the situation.

86   *Balance Empathy and Action*

What was the situation?

List three to five emotions that you felt. Don't just write a single word. Instead of "fear," write "afraid that I would lose my father." Instead of "angry," write "angry that my ideas weren't being heard."

How did the emotions affect you? How you thought of yourself? Of others? How did it change the way you saw the situation?

It is this last piece, the effect feelings have on you, that is the key to empathy. You don't just have feelings; they have you. When you are listening to a protégé who is in the grip of his feelings, connect both with the emo-tion itself and with how debilitating it can leave you. Then, realize how powerful it can be to have someone who shares this feeling, making you feel less alone with it.

> You don't just have feelings; they have you.

Take a Step Back

To this point, I have focused on drawing out the emotions that are keeping the protégé from moving forward. Shining a spotlight on the protégé's feelings helps to both identify what is blocking progress and let the protégé know someone cares about her. At this point, it could be easy to get drawn into the emotional feedback cycle and begin to wallow with the protégé. It is at this point that the "balance" that is at the heart of this rule comes into play.

The next step is to begin to lessen the grip the emotions have on the situation and begin to move toward action. It can be difficult to see if a protégé is ready to move beyond the feelings conversation. There won't be a red light that goes off announcing a readiness to explore options. Rather, you will need to tactfully test your protégé for a readiness to move forward. There are several ways to check for readiness.

Balance Empathy and Action 87

The easiest can be to ask straight out: "I can tell that this problem is really bothering you. I've been there, too. I'm wondering if there is anything you can do about it? Do you want to talk about options? Or, do we have more exploring to do?" Asking the question directly after the emotions have been explored creates opportunity to pivot to the head side of the issue, opening the door to your insight questions. It is important to ask the question in such a way that leaves the door open to further exploration of the emotional side. Hurrying the protégé back to the rational side of the issue prematurely might cause you to wind up back where Amanda found herself at the beginning of the chapter: with a protégé who doesn't feel understood.

Another approach to testing for readiness is through a technique called Feel, Felt, Found. The basic notion is to validate the protégé's feelings (Feel), connect with the protégé through your own feelings (Felt), and give the protégé some perspective that helps him take the step back (Found).

For example, your protégé, Norm, is struggling with what he believes is a generational issue with one of his direct reports. He has a hard time connecting with Robin and motivating her to focus on what he thinks should be top priority. He leaves meetings **Feel,** with her frustrated because he thinks she is dismissing his **Felt,** guidance as old and out of touch. She wants to commu- **Found** nicate over email or texting, whereas he prefers a face-to-face meeting. Norm has thrown up his hands and said, "There is nothing I can do with Robin; the generational gap between us is too wide." After exploring Norm's frustrations a bit, you can help him take step back through your own experience:

Feel: Norm, I can see this situation with Robin has you very frustrated. You **feel** like nothing you do is getting through to her and that you cannot find a common ground.

Felt: I **felt** this way with one of my subordinates, Rich. He and I seemed to be from different planets, and I didn't know how to motivate him. I felt like giving up on him because of the generational distance between us.

Found: I'm glad I didn't give up, because I **found** that he and I were motivated by different things. What I had attributed to a generational difference was really just a difference in what drove us to work. I was motivated by working long hours and feeling like I was getting things done. He was more motivated by praise and feedback than I was. I had thought his difference was due to our age gap, but I recognized that others of my generation were motivated by praise just as others of his generation were motivated by long hours. Seeing it this way helped me find a better path forward with him.

88   *Balance Empathy and Action*

This brief exposition into one of your stories helps your protégé connect with you and take a perspective that shows there may be some resolution to the issue. Using Feel, Felt, Found validates the protégé's feelings, makes him or her feel understood, and opens the conversation up to considering options that hadn't been considered before.

One final way to begin to move to action is to help the protégé evaluate the situation in light of her overall goals and values. We can often find ourselves in the grips of a situation that may be very important in the present, but has little impact on our longer-term goals. We can spend a lot of energy wrapped up in the present and losing sight of the larger journey we are on. Part of the reason mentors need to chart a course up front is to help you find out the protégé's bigger priorities. Knowing the protégé's larger aspirations and goals gives you a tool to establish perspective with her.

If you return to Norm, you could go one way by asking, "Norm, how can you think about this situation with Robin in light of your longer-term goal of becoming a better leader? Do you think the issue you have with her could come up again? Would there be value in trying to figure out this situation as part of your overall development as a leader?" Helping Norm see the situation with Robin as part of his overall growth could help him get a different perspective on the situation, which would stimulate more problem solving.

On the other hand, you could go the other way by asking, "Norm, I realize that you are struggling with your relationship with Robin. I know that it really bothers you, but I'm wondering if it is taking up more of your time than it should. When we first met, we talked about how you wanted to get more comfortable around senior leaders as you work toward your next promotion. While the situation with Robin can be frustrating, do you want to shift how we spend our time back to talking about your original goals?" In this example, you are calling attention to the situation with Robin as a distraction to Norm's longer-term goals. Time spent dwelling on Robin is taking away from progress Norm could be making on his longer journey.

In either case, you are helping to establish perspective with the protégé. By either connecting the situation to the goals, or shifting the focus back to longer-term goals, you are helping to lessen the grip the situation currently has on the protégé's emotional energy.

Overcoming Inertia

Up until this point, we have been discussing how protégés struggle with emotions that cloud their thinking about the situation. The emotions are getting in the way of the protégé thinking clearly about the situation and finding a path forward. For those emotions, the mentor is trying to

Balance Empathy and Action 89

create a safe place for the protégé to express their feelings in order to lessen their power. When the emotion has been released, the protégé can approach the situation as a head issue and start to discuss options for solving it.

Sometimes, the heart issue confronting a protégé is not the emotions clouding his thinking. Rather, he has an idea of what will need to change to improve the situation, but he is not taking steps to move forward. He is stuck in the inertia of the status quo. The heart issue is the fear of making a significant change. More specifically, the protégé is afraid of the risk that comes with upsetting the status quo of his current situation, even if the situation is causing him pain or is not what he would want. Inertia is created by a complex set of thoughts and feelings that keep a protégé from making a change that disrupts his world. As was noted in the last rule, most of us want things to stay the same but get better.

Jack was a junior partner at a mid-sized law firm where he had worked for nine years. While he billed enough hours to be made a partner, he was very uncomfortable doing business development. As a result, he was dependent on some of the firm's rainmakers to stay busy. Les was one of those rainmakers. He was always developing business and giving it out to associates and other partners to keep their time sheets full. While Jack and the others were grateful for Les's largesse, they all found him a pain to deal with. Les wanted constant updates on his work, asking Jack to respond to texts and emails at all hours of the night. "It would not be so bad if they truly were things that couldn't wait until morning," Jack said. "Les gets as angry if you ignore the small stuff he asks for as he does for the big things." The other problem was, Les would treat you like his best friend until he didn't. If you let Les down, he would cut you off from new work for months at a time to let you know he was disappointed.

Jack and Scott, a senior partner and Jack's mentor at the firm, spent many hours talking about Jack's struggles dealing with Les. While Scott knew of Les, the firm was big enough that he didn't know him very well. As Scott listened to Jack's stories, he was astounded by how poorly Les was treating Jack. He also knew that Les wasn't the last partner like this Jack would encounter and that Jack needed to find a way to solve his own situation. At first, Scott believed Jack had a traditional heart issue and that empathizing with him and letting him vent would help him see a path forward. Over time, however, Scott began to realize there was a lot more that was keeping Jack from breaking the inertia of his situation with Les. He started to see the signs in Jack that let him know there was more at stake.

Working on Symptoms. First of all, Jack would spend a lot of time talking through tactics he could change to avoid Les's ire. "Maybe I could

90   *Balance Empathy and Action*

turn my phone off at night," was one idea that was offered and quickly discarded. "What if I set aside 10:00 to 11:00 p.m. every night to respond to Les's requests," was another idea. Scott was scratching at the periphery of the issue, trying to avoid anything that would require him to directly deal with Les. While not always a sure sign that a protégé is stuck in inertia, a protégé who spends time working on symptoms or low-hanging fruit instead of getting to the core of an issue tells you this change will be difficult.

Giving up Quickly. Scott also saw Jack taking small steps, but then backing off of them quickly. One idea Jack came up with was to route Les's emails into a mailbox that he wouldn't look at until 7:30 a.m. every day. Scott thought it was a fair strategy and encouraged Jack to give it a try. At their next mentoring meeting, Scott asked how it was going. "I stuck with it for a week, and everything seemed fine. Then, on Sunday night the second week, Les asked for an update on a deposition I was preparing for the next morning. When I didn't reply, he started texting me until I called him and said I would work on it that night. So, I guess that strategy didn't work." While Scott was a little disappointed that Jack gave up that quickly, he was seeing the trend in Jack's approach to the issue.

Resist Exploring Substantive Options. After the deposition issue, Scott asked a few questions to test whether Jack wanted to talk about the core issues. He started with, "I'm wondering if the email strategy was too subtle for Les. What could you do to be more explicit about redefining your relationship?"

"Confront him? I couldn't do that! I need the hours on my timesheet too much," came Jack's reply.

"What about other partners? Have you tried to get work from some of them?" Scott asked.

"They all have associates they work with. Plus, Les practices the kind of law I really enjoy," Jack replied.

Scott tried one more idea. "This might be a longer-term strategy, but maybe we could start talking about more business development so that you aren't as dependent on Les?"

"I don't know. Maybe," Jack said as he sank in his chair. "I just wish I could have an evening when I didn't dread hearing my phone pinging at me."

Scott realized that Jack had lost the belief and desire to change his situation. There was something that was sustaining his inertia that they hadn't discovered. He recognized that Jack wasn't ready to move to action yet, and there was more work to do in understanding Jack's situation.

Sources of Inertia

With any substantial change, there are usually several factors that are supporting the status quo. Many of them are based in fear: fear of disrupting a situation I know and (at some level) have made peace with; fear of doing something different that may not work (or make things worse); fear of upsetting relationships; or fear of letting go of beliefs. Understanding these sources as a mentor can guide you in your approach to discussing them with your protégé. Doing so also helps you empathize a bit more, as you may have been stuck in your own inertia for similar reasons. Let's briefly examine each of these fears.

Fear of Leaving Here. Jack desperately wants to change his situation with Les, but he fears upsetting the current balance. Right now, he gets work from Les and is (sometimes) able to keep Les happy. In Jack's mental calculus of his situation, he may be in a net positive. While Les creates a lot of anguish for him, he is, on balance, in a situation he can live with. Well, that he can live with most days. In fact, if he were to track his net happiness with his situation over time, he probably would recognize that the situation with Les has deteriorated, and he is actually in a much worse place than he was when things started. On the other hand, it is a situation he knows, and it can be difficult for anyone to venture away from a pain he knows into an unknown. Fear will trump pain most days of the week.

> Fear will trump pain most days of the week.

Beyond the fear of upsetting his current situation, he also recognizes that he has more at stake than just his relationship with Les. If things go badly when he tries to make a significant change with Les, his mind travels to some of the worst case scenarios: he might make an enemy of Les, who has a big network in the local legal community. Worse, he might lose his job at the law firm, one he needs to pay his bills and support his family. Many of us will tolerate difficult, painful circumstances because of some larger factors that are at stake that the current situation provides.

Finally, there is the situation of "spinning plates." Imagine a circus performer who is trying to keep multiple plates spinning in the air, running between them to keep them going. Les is only one part of all of the demands on Jack; he is only one plate. He may also have to deal with a few difficult to manage clients. There may be other partners who, while not as bad as Les, need their own attention. He may also be a new father and is trying to balance demands at home with demands at work. Jack, like many protégés who take on a lot of responsibility, may have many plates spinning in the air. While the Les plate may be

92 *Balance Empathy and Action*

a problem, he at least has it under enough control that he can worry about the other plates.

Fear of Going There. Even if your protégé decides that the situation has deteriorated enough that he is willing to risk changing the current situation, there is always the fear of the new. What if Jack tries to stand up to Les? What if it doesn't work? What if standing up to him makes the situation worse? While the promise of a better situation can be encouraging, there is no guarantee that things will work out. Furthermore, the envisioned future is conceptual while the practical reality is concrete. Jack has to calculate whether he is willing to trade what he knows for what he doesn't know. He has to assess the likelihood of successfully changing his situation against the risk of it not working out. His doubts about being able to meaningfully change his situation will rob him of the energy he needs to overcome the inertia.

Fear of Upsetting Relationships. Taking a step back further, you can see all of the actors around Jack who have a vested interest in the status quo. Things are clearly working for Les (as far as he can tell), so he will work against Jack trying to change the situation. But, there are also the other associates who appreciate the fact that Jack absorbs some of Les's attention. While they may sympathize with him, they may be thinking, "Better him than me." There are Les's other partners who don't want to confront the reality of how he treats associates for fear of upsetting him and putting all of the work he brings into the firm at risk. Unless he can find an ally to support him challenging his situation, Jack may find a lot of forces lined up against him.

Fear of Letting Go of Beliefs. The last fear that keeps any of us from meaningful change is the fear of letting go of our beliefs. Each of us carries around a set of concepts about how the world works. More to the point, we have beliefs about how the world *should* work: Hard work should be rewarded. Bullies should be punished. Leaders should not stand idly by and tolerate the bad behavior of one of their own. When Scott asks Jack what he can do to change his situation, Jack might fire back, "I'm not doing anything wrong. Why should I have to change? Les is the one you should be asking that!" It is often our own beliefs about how the world should work that keeps us from making meaningful change. This fact does not mean that we should not hold values or beliefs that guide us. It just means that some of our beliefs are more black and white when the reality is far more nuanced than we would like to believe.

In the end, the status quo is a powerful, self-correcting force. We all seek harmony and equilibrium in our relationships. Life will never be perfect, and we always have to make compromises to keep the peace. These are the forces against which change struggles. In order to make change

Balance Empathy and Action   93

in your own world, you are not only fighting your own vested interest in the status quo, you are also disrupting others' equilibrium, and they will work to put things back the way they were.

Breaking Through

With all of that said, change happens all of the time. Every day people are breaking their own cycles of inertia and improving their lives for the better. Many do so with the help of a mentor who believes in them. While you cannot create the change for your protégé, you can provide the support that gives her the confidence to take the risks needed to create real change.

When you see a protégé being held in place by inertia, start with **empathy**. Use the exercise from earlier in the chapter to connect with your own feelings when you were facing a change that was very difficult to make. Focus on one that challenged you for some time. Recall what that felt like, especially at a low point when you felt helpless about your situation. Your protégé may be feeling that way now. Even if you don't share how you felt at that time with your protégé (after all, the protégé's situation isn't about you), use those feelings to empathize with how your protégé may be feeling.

In addition to connecting through empathy, you also want to reinforce the **safe place** you are creating for your protégé. One big part of the safe place for exploring inertia is to avoid judging your protégé. She may be embarrassed about being in her predicament. Being judged by her mentor will make her feel worse and damage the trust the two of you have built. If you feel yourself beginning to judge your protégé, go back to your own inertia situation. Imagine talking about your situation with a trusted mentor, looking for a supportive environment that gives you some hope or at least respite. Now imagine that mentor saying to you, "That is ridiculous. If I were in your situation, I wouldn't tolerate that." Whenever you start to feel that way about your protégé, think about that and return to empathy.

Look for opportunities to give your protégé **hope**. When your protégé has no belief that she can change her situation, she won't take meaningful action to break her cycle of inertia. Tell stories of your own struggles and what it took to get through them. You may be able to highlight bright spots that point to a path forward. Even if that path is nowhere to be found, remind her that things will get better at some point and that you still believe in her.

Finally, you want to remember to **lead by following**. This situation is your protégé's, not yours. It is not your problem to solve. You are here acting as a guide, confidant, and counselor. She needs to go through the struggle just as you have gone through your own struggles. As

94 *Balance Empathy and Action*

much as you want to take away her pain and alleviate her suffering, you cannot take over and solve her problems for her. She will get through this on her own schedule. Focus on being the mentor that she needs right now.

Taking Time

With all heart issues, you need to exercise patience. Exploring the feelings side of any heart issue can take an emotional toll on a protégé, and he may not be in the mental frame of mind to start looking at options yet. He may need some time to let the emotions subside before he is ready to talk about it again. You may need to wrap up a mentoring conversation leaving the issue unresolved to give the protégé time to recover. Remember that mentoring is a process, and processes take time.

Rather than leave the issue entirely, I would recommend you give the protégé some homework to complete before you meet again (more on homework in the next rule, Foster Accountability). Ask the protégé to put aside thirty minutes to answer the following three questions:

1. What are all of the feelings that you are experiencing because of this issue? (You may want to give your protégé a copy of the list from earlier in the chapter.)

2. What have you tried to do about the situation so far? What were the results of the different tactics you have attempted? What have you thought of but haven't tried yet?

3. If you could find a solution to the issue, what would that be worth to you? How would things be better if you could solve it?

Balance Empathy and Action 95

The last question is laying the groundwork for creating energy to find a solution. You are getting the protégé to see the larger benefits of working toward a solution which will likely outweigh the short-term emotions the protégé is feeling now. Make sure you ask the protégé about the homework at the next meeting. Use that meeting to explore the emotions, going through each one the protégé wrote down. Then, explore the options the protégé has tried to see what paths have been attempted and which haven't. Finally, use the answer to the last questions to start to build energy toward taking action and moving forward with the protégé.

7 Foster Accountability

"Thanks again for your time. I always enjoy our discussions. I'll ask Jennifer to put another meeting on your calendar for next month," Finbar said as he left Martina's office.

Martina sat back and smiled to herself. She had also enjoyed her talks with Finbar over the last six months ever since he asked her to be his mentor. He always had interesting things to discuss, and she liked seeing things from his perspective. She also liked the feeling that she was really helping someone who had a lot of energy and enthusiasm.

She turned to her tablet to add to her notes she kept from their meetings. After finishing the notes from this meeting, she began to review the notes from their prior meetings. Her brow furrowed slightly as she read over the eight entries in her log. At the end of each entry, she had recorded one or two things that Finbar said he wanted to do before their next meeting. One item caught her eye, mostly because it was at the end of each of their meetings: "Set up a ride-along with sales reps to learn more about how the customers use our products." His overall mentoring goals were focused on learning more broadly about the business so he could advance his career. Finbar worked in R&D, and felt very disconnected from the customers for whom he was designing products. He mentioned how much he would like to get out into the field a few times to get a better idea of how the end users interacted with the product as well as learn how they made their purchasing decisions. Martina and Finbar agreed (several times, it would seem) that he could easily accomplish this by going on some ride-alongs with several of the sales reps that reported up through Martina.

In fact, they had agreed to this course of action after every meeting. Martina had even called one of her managers to set up a meeting for Finbar so he could arrange some ride-alongs. Looking back on her notes, she realized that he hadn't followed up on any of the action items they had discussed. While she really enjoyed talking to Finbar, she realized that he wasn't making any tangible progress on his goals. She put her tablet down and sat forward in her chair, staring at the empty chair in front of her desk. "He hasn't really done anything," she whispered to herself. "Am I really helping him?"

Martina's situation is far from unique. Having a mentor presents a tremendous opportunity for individual growth. Yet, many protégés fail to capitalize on the power mentoring brings. They get the comfort that comes from having a friend, and perspective that a more senior individual brings. But, the real benefit of mentoring comes from turning words into action. Finbar was leaving a lot of value on the table by failing to take action on the topics that he and Martina discussed.

Mentoring, after all, is about learning. Mentors are guides along a journey of learning and discovery for protégés. While the conventional definition of learning involves the acquisition of knowledge, psychologists define learning as a relatively permanent change in behavior that comes from experience. It is the application of that knowledge on a consistent basis that indicates that one has learned. It is the difference between knowing what should be done and doing it.

Noel Burch of Gordon Training International devised a four-step learning model that would be helpful here (Adams, 2011). The model describes how we pass through phases of not knowing something to mastering it to the extent that it feels natural:

1. **Unconscious incompetence.** The protégé does not know something and does not recognize that knowing or doing it would make things better. That is, there is some deficit but the protégé does not recognize that she could do something differently to close it. In the example above, Finbar had moved past this phase. He recognized his gap and knew that he could take some steps to close it.
2. **Conscious incompetence.** The protégé recognizes the gap and is taking steps to close it. This phase may involve learning through discussion, reading, observing, or practice. It can be a time of trial and error to find out what works and how to do it. Finbar was stuck on this step, as many protégés are; he kept talking about what he should do but wasn't taking any steps to close the gap.
3. **Conscious competence.** At this phase, the protégé has learned how to do something, but the learning can still be tenuous and fragile. It requires conscious effort to use the skill, and the protégé can easily slip backward into old habits.
4. **Unconscious competence.** The final phase of learning is marked by a protégé who not only knows something but does it without thinking. The learning has been woven into the fabric of his being and comes naturally. Old habits have been replaced with new ones and the knowledge has been mastered.

In prior chapters, we focused on transitioning from the first to the second phase. The focus was on creating a safe environment where a protégé could explore the gaps and discover solutions to his challenges. In this chapter, we turn the corner from the second phase through the third

Foster Accountability

phase of learning. The mentor is helping the protégé not only experiment with new ways of doing things but also to make the change permanent. Some of the most powerful and gratifying mentoring can come about when you create accountability that helps the protégé through the difficult process of learning and change.

Before continuing, I want to point out that this perspective on mentoring is not meant to diminish or indict your prior mentors if they didn't play such an active role for you. Many positive mentoring relationships are not as active as the ones that have been described in this book. For instance, I described my relationship with Bro. Feld in the first chapter of the book. I was probably just one of a countless line of students to him, but one encounter with him where he challenged me changed how I thought about myself at the time. That meeting didn't end with action items or another meeting on the calendar. But, what it did do for me was initiate action for me. It caused me to set a higher bar for myself, to apply myself more, and to begin habits that carried me through graduate school and into my career. He touched a nerve that spurred my own action. Moments like these with a mentor are precious and rare.

> A mentor is a catalyst for change.

Think back to your mentors who had a significant impact on you. What did you do differently as a result of your relationship with them? What changed in how you see yourself and what you did as a result? A mentor is a catalyst for change. Some protégés will recognize the opportunity to grow that mentoring presents and take advantage of the energy mentoring creates within them. Many others, however, will view the work of growth as one more task to complete. And, it is a task that typically no one else is asking about, especially compared to bosses and others who are asking about the other, more immediate tasks. As a mentor, you cannot force your protégé to see the opportunity and act on it. But, you can create an environment that enables action and nudges your protégé out of her comfort zone and toward growth. Growing (and changing) can be a long process. Having a mentor who is there to create some accountability can make the process easier.

Trust, Goals, and Accountability

Martina and Finbar have what appears to be a very positive relationship. They have built a platform of trust that allows Finbar to open up and explore issues that are important to him. They also have a direction to their discussions that is guided by his overall goals. There is a critical third ingredient that is missing, however, that is causing their partnership to flounder a bit: accountability. He steps up to the boundary between the first and second phases of learning, but doesn't

Foster Accountability 99

cross it. Martina has the opportunity to draw him across the boundary by using accountability.

The idea of a mentor holding a protégé accountable may feel somewhat unnatural in a mentoring partnership. Creating accountability is a boss's job, after all, not a mentor's. The accountability a mentor creates is different, however, than what a boss does. The boss is typically focused on the protégé's responsibilities, which typically have deadlines and sometimes consequences if they are not fulfilled. The boss usually holds power over the protégé, including positional power and often some degree of financial power (for example, the ability to grant raises, bonuses, or even continued employment).

A mentor's accountability is significantly different. It is more subtle and less threatening. It comes from more of a relationship basis, where the protégé doesn't want to let a mentor down. While many positive manager–subordinate relationships are defined similarly, even the most supportive boss still holds formal authority over the protégé and therefore establishes a different dynamic. When a mentor asks if a protégé was able to complete a task, the question doesn't carry with it an implied "And if you didn't, it goes on your annual performance evaluation." When the mentor asks the same question, it is out of support and interest in the protégé.

Think of a mentor's relationship to your career goals in the same way you think of a personal trainer's relationship with your fitness goals. When your alarm goes off at 5:00 a.m. for your appointment at the gym with your trainer, you may be tempted to hit snooze and skip the gym today. But, you realize that doing so would let down your trainer, and you know she or he would ask you about it. You think to yourself, *It's just easier to get up and go to the gym than explain it to Joe the Trainer.* But, Joe the Trainer can't give you a negative performance evaluation or tell you that you're not getting a raise for not going to the gym. In fact, you are in control of the relationship with Joe just as your protégé is in control of her relationship with you. You have hired Joe *because* he will get you to go to the gym instead of hitting snooze on your alarm. A mentor helps you keep from hitting snooze on your career.

One of my own protégés had an action item on her to do list for much of our partnership during the mentoring program in which we were enrolled. The action item was part of her career goals and was very important to her. But, it also was very scary. She didn't want to do it, but she knew she needed to, so she asked me to hold her accountable for it. In fact, the year-long program came to an end without her achieving it. Every meeting, she said that she hadn't completed that item, and that she was sorry and felt embarrassed. I fostered accountability by asking about it, but not in the way a boss would. She wouldn't get a negative evaluation on her annual performance review from me; we didn't even work at the same consulting firm. But, she felt the subtle pressure of letting down

100 *Foster Accountability*

a mentor. In fact, when the program came to an end, she asked if she could schedule another meeting so that she could take care of that action item and clear her conscience (about three months after the end of the program, she completed the final task).

In its own way, creating accountability is a way to show that you are interested in your protégé and that you care. You know what your protégé's goals are, and you believe in her. You want her to succeed. She feels like you are in her corner and that she isn't alone.

Start by Asking

Fostering accountability always begins with a question. When you are finishing a meeting, ask what steps your protégé could take between now and the next meeting based on your conversation. Research demonstrates that when someone tells someone else about their future behavioral intentions, they are more likely to follow through on them (Gollwitzer and Sheeran, 2006). In this sense, Martina was performing half of the accountability task by asking Finbar what he was going to do after their meetings.

Unfortunately, she did not take the second step of beginning the next meeting with the action steps. When you have a meeting with a protégé, pull out your notes from the last meeting and review what steps the protégé said she or he was going to take. In the meeting, after you have caught up and identified any goals the protégé has for the meeting, say, "I'd also like to hear how you did with your action items from the last meeting." The power of accountability shows through in this second step. The list of action steps from the last meeting transforms from a conceptual list of things she *ought to* do to something her mentor is going to ask about. The accountability is subtle, and the only negative consequence to the protégé is the fear of disappointing a mentor. But, if there is a relationship that is built on trust and respect, the fear of disappointment becomes a powerful motivator.

As a mentor, you want to be careful not to abuse this power. Leveraging guilt too much can lead to the protégé resenting the mentor and cause the mentor–protégé relationship to degrade over time. When you ask the protégé, you want to do it in a supportive way instead of one that makes it seem like you are checking up on the protégé. Starting with, "Okay, you said you were going to read that article and schedule a meeting with Ravi. Did you do that?" would probably make the protégé react with some defensiveness. However, starting with, "Last time you said you were going to read an article and meet with Ravi. I'm wondering if you made progress with those items" is more supportive.

What you are trying to avoid is the perception that the protégé is being judged. Part of creating a safe place is keeping judgment at bay. When the

Foster Accountability 101

protégé feels that you are judging him, he starts to lose a little trust in you and your relationship. The fear of disappointing a mentor can become laced with guilt and shame, negative emotions that infect the relationship and put distance between the two of you. Keeping judgment out of your relationship begins with keeping it out of your head.

When Martina realized that Finbar hadn't followed through on what seemed to her to be a relatively simple task, her mind began filling with judgments of him: He doesn't really care about this goal. He is too lazy to follow through. He is all talk and no action. Judgments like those are a natural reaction when we are facing a situation we do not understand. However, they create problems for a mentor because they usually show up in the questions we ask, either in the words we use or the way we ask them, or both. When you find judgments about your protégé filling your head, stop and say this to yourself: *My protégé is a smart, motivated person. I wonder what is getting in the way of taking the next step.* This question can help your change your mindset from judgment to inquiry. With this new mindset, you can start to help your protégé with the next step in fostering accountability: finding the barrier.

Finding the Barrier(s)

"Finbar, I noticed that we have talked about setting up a ride-along at the end of several meetings, but it doesn't sound like you have set it up yet. Do you want to talk about what might be getting in your way?" By opening the dialogue without judgment and an inquiring mindset, Martina is inviting Finbar to explore what is keeping him from taking the action that he says he wants to take. If handled in a supportive, judgment-free way, they might be able to discover where he is encountering a barrier (or barriers, as there may be more than one).

First of all, the protégé is **not prioritizing** the action over other things. This issue arises often because the mentoring conversation seems like a time and space disconnected from the real world of responsibility. How many times have you attended a workshop or retreat and left with a lot of great intentions, but all of that evaporates when you get back to work? What seemed like a great idea when talking to her mentor becomes just one more thing to do. And, since all of the other activities have people expecting them to be done, the action drops to the bottom of the priority list. The forces of inertia we examined in the last chapter need extra force to overcome them. The new action needs conscious priority placed on it to break through the inertia.

Other times, a task that sounds simple when discussing with a mentor is **more complicated** or time-consuming than originally thought. For instance, say your protégé would benefit from taking a class in having difficult conversations. On its surface, that sounds easy: sign

102 *Foster Accountability*

up for the class and go. But, the task itself may have many parts, such as (a) getting permission from a boss to take the class and spend the money for the class, (b) finding a date on the schedule that would work, and (c) scheduling other things around it. Many tasks are even more complicated that that. Help your protégé by breaking more complicated tasks down to simpler sub-tasks and focusing on the next step, as David Allen (2015) suggests in his book *Getting Things Done: The Art of Stress-Free Productivity*.

A third possibility is that the task that seemed important in one meeting has **dropped in importance** later. It may be that accomplishing the task is not as important to the goal it supports than other things that could be done. Or, the goal to which it was tied has dropped in priority relative to other goals. If either of these is the case, it would be best to drop the task and find some other action the protégé could take that would have more impact on the important goals.

Finally, many protégés postpone taking steps that are important to accomplishing their goals because the **fear of what they need to do** is more tangible and present than the perceived benefit of accomplishing the goal. For example, your protégé wants to become more comfortable speaking in public, so you recommend signing up for a speaker's club like Toastmasters. While getting time on the schedule to attend a meeting may be easy, the fear of attending the meeting (where the protégé may be asked to speak in public) may overpower the desire to complete the task. The desire to get comfortable speaking in public takes a backseat to the fear of doing so.

The last barrier is often the most difficult to determine, because protégés often do not want to admit the fear to a mentor. Instead, the lack of progress on the task masquerades as the problems above (for example, "I don't have time"). Care must be taken, as forcing the protégé to admit to the fear may strain the trust that has been developed. Addressing it directly by saying, "I think you're letting your fears keep you from doing what you know you need to do" will likely put a protégé back on his heels and elicit a defensive response. You may consider trying, "It seems like there may be something getting in the way of you taking action. I'm wondering if your fear of speaking in public is keeping you from attending that meeting."

When you are seeing a protégé stall in forward progress, take time to slow down and explore what may be getting in the way. Remember that you may have been in a similar spot yourself when you were blocked from pursuing your own goals. Use your empathy to connect with the protégé and talk about how you have overcome your own hurdles in the past. At the end of the day, you want to focus on maintaining your mentoring partnership as a safe place for the protégé, free from judgment. The greatest gift you have to offer is your own care and concern.

Changing Habits

Finding and overcoming barriers is only the first step toward the "relatively permanent change in behavior" that shows growth and learning. Taking the first step is important, as it represents the transition from Conscious Incompetence to Conscious Competence. For some issues, the first steps will carry the protégé forward as they encounter success with the new actions they are taking. These successes in turn reinforce the behavior to the point that it becomes easier and automatic.

For other issues, particularly complex head and heart issues, the protégé is facing another source of inertia: his own habits. He might try a different approach to the situation one time and be pleased with the results. But, one win may not be enough to overcome habits that have built up over years. That is the barrier hidden in Conscious Competence: the protégé has to think about the new behavior, which takes mental effort. The new behavior is battling years of doing it another way that may feel more natural.

Nari had been promoted to director in her company's regulatory affairs function. Her Ph.D. in chemistry and her MBA meant she loved to analyze problems. While this skill served her well in her earlier roles, it was tripping her up now. When faced with a difficult decision, she would dig into the issue and get lost in the details. She even found herself reanalyzing recommendations that her managers brought her to make sure she was comfortable. She quickly became a bottleneck, slowing down decisions all around her.

She and her mentor, Wayland, had worked on what to do when she felt the temptation to go deeper on analysis than the decision needed, giving her questions to ask her managers that would ensure their recommendations were sound without getting drawn into the analysis herself. She tried it for a few weeks and found that it worked very well. But, when the pace and stress of work started to pile up, she found herself giving into her old habits. Wayland thought that Nari had turned the corner, so he stopped asking her about it. In fact, it wasn't until two months later, after Nari met with her vice president who told her she was back to her old ways, that they realized that Nari's old habits had taken over.

It can be difficult to change habits, especially when they have been reinforced over time. Nari had been successful in prior years for the exact tendencies that were tripping her up now. During the Conscious Competence phase of learning, the protégé is susceptible to falling backwards under times of stress when resources are low. Not only did Nari need to learn the new behaviors, she needed to recognize when they were needed. As Charles Duhigg noted in his book *The Power of Habit* (2012), she needed to identify the cues that told her she had to use the new behaviors. She also needed Wayland to ask her about it beyond the first few weeks of success she had. In fact, talking through her success would help

104   *Foster Accountability*

cement the new routine in her mind and move her in the direction of Unconscious Competence.

Not every issue your protégé faces will need this level of support. There are two cues to look for that signal the need for support during Conscious Competence: 1. Your protégé struggles to find her way through the barrier; and, 2. The habit she is trying to change has been reinforced for years, especially when it has led to success in the past. In these instances, you can foster accountability to help make the learning last.

Failure and Learning

The road to growth and learning is rarely smooth. There will always be setbacks along the way. In fact, failing is a natural part of learning. As we venture beyond our comfort zone into what psychologists call the Zone of Proximal Development (ZPD: Vygotsky, 1978), we are by definition in uncharted territory. We are trying new things, learning new behaviors, observing the new results we achieve. Mistakes and failure are a natural part of the process. In fact, if you aren't making mistakes, you might question whether you are really learning.

> Negative results are just what I want. They're just as valuable to me as positive results. I can never find the thing that does the job best until I find the ones that don't.
> —Thomas A. Edison

When actively learning new things and developing Conscious Competence, your protégé has entered the struggle that we discussed in the rule Lead by Following. Learning can be a hard-fought process that will see setbacks and frustrations. As a mentor, you can help ease your protégé's way, but you cannot do the work for him. Martina, our mentor from the beginning of the chapter, could have easily sat down with Finbar and talked to him about their customers, how she sees them using the company's product, and shared her own insights with him. But, that would have been no substitute for him doing the work himself. He also needed to be free to make mistakes as he learned, as those mistakes will contain powerful lessons that will cement his learning.

If you are going to truly help your protégé learn, you want to create an environment where the protégé is not afraid of making mistakes. You may not want to send your protégé out into the world with the encouragement, "Go make some good mistakes today!" But, you may want to say, "Go try doing some new things, or try doing some old things in new ways! Then, come back and tell me what worked, what didn't, and what you learned." You want to extend the safe place you have created to envelop the ZPD where your protégé feels comfortable exploring and learning.

Foster Accountability 105

You want your protégé to realize that the fear of failing is usually worse than failing itself. Fear of making mistakes is not necessarily a bad thing. It keeps us from blurting out thoughts that pop into our heads during meetings and causes us to think twice about sending that vicious email response. The fear gets in the way, however, when it is applied uniformly to all mistakes instead of separating good mistakes from bad ones.

One lesson you should teach your protégé is, all mistakes are not created equally. Some mistakes should be avoided while others should be embraced. Some are discouraging while others are energizing. They should all be approached with an appreciation for what they can teach you, as failure begets learning and growth. Help your protégé separate different types of mistakes and appreciate them for what they can teach.

Experimental mistakes. One set of mistakes we make is when we are trying truly new things. We are doing things we haven't done before, and we are bound to make mistakes. Think of what would happen if Finbar finally scheduled his ride-along. He might pepper the sales rep with all sorts of questions that even the greenest sales rep would know. In a meeting with a customer, he might start asking about the competitor's product and what the customer liked or disliked about it. While these actions might cause the sales rep to cringe, they represent Finbar getting outside of his comfort zone and exploring.

Experimental mistakes provide an opportunity for rapid learning. After his first ride-along, Martina should spend time discussing the experience with Finbar. They can explore the insights he got from the experience (for example, that even price-conscious buyers have a certain level of quality they expect) as well as what he learned about interacting with customers (such as, some can get uncomfortable when being asked pointed questions). By setting aside time with Finbar shortly after his experience, Martina is also capitalizing on the energy that comes from his new learning and using it to reinforce further experimentation. Finally, she can help him see that the ride-along he had avoided setting up was not as bad as he had feared.

Stretch mistakes. The skills Nari is learning are much more complex. There are several components to what she is trying to accomplish. She wants to be cognizant of when she feels tempted to take over something from one of her subordinates. She also needs to work on trusting them more and identify what keeps her from trusting them. In addition, she needs to examine the standards she sets for herself and see if she is setting the bar too high for her subordinates. That is not to imply that she shouldn't have high standards; rather, she and Wayland should examine whether the effort needed to get her subordinates to her level of perfection (99%) is worth the incremental benefit over where they are (95%).

The mistakes Nari will be making are more complex than those Finbar is. He is learning new things and experimenting with what will and won't work for him. In addition to learning to do new things (e.g., coach her

106   *Foster Accountability*

subordinates through a task), she is also unlearning old habits that had worked for her in the past (e.g., do the task herself). Instead of merely climbing a new learning curve, she is likely to see a performance decline in the near term as she lets go of what had been working in the past to learn what will work better going forward. During this Conscious Competence phase of learning, the temptation to go back to old habits is even stronger because of the dip in results that will likely occur. This pattern is what happened to Nari and Wayland. Because she started to make progress, he stopped focusing on the learning. When she made mistakes with her new coaching style, she reverted to her old habits rather than learn from the mistakes.

When describing how to support someone achieving stretch goals, David Yeager recommends giving "wise feedback," which is a mixture of high standards with belief that the protégé can perform and reach the goals (Yeager et al., 2013). As you recall from the prior chapter, protégés need a mixture of belief and desire to succeed. Wise feedback addresses both halves of this equation. Wayland can maintain high standards with Nari by asking her about how she is progressing, which will stoke her desire to perform. If she knows he will be asking about it, she is more motivated to follow through. In addition, his stated belief that she can perform can undergird her own belief in herself. Yeager's research found that after a failed attempt, wise feedback had a significant impact on whether the subject made a second attempt. That is, the mixture of high standards with assurance that the giver of feedback believed in the subject resulted in making a secondary effort instead of accepting the failure. Had Wayland continued to ask Nari about her coaching, she would have been more likely to stick with it even when she encountered the inevitable setbacks that come with growth and learning.

Careless mistakes. The last type of mistake is the careless one. These are the mistakes we make every day when we aren't thinking about what we are doing. They can be as simple as forgetting to attach an important document to an email to as disastrous as crashing a car while distracted. While most careless mistakes are somewhat random and don't rise to the level of a mentoring conversation, there are two instances when you may want to explore them with your protégé. First, look for patterns in careless mistakes that could reveal a larger, underlying issue. One such careless mistake could be "forgetting" to invite a difficult customer to project review meetings. The customer usually asks difficult questions and causes more work to come out of the meetings. The forgetfulness could indicate a more difficult issue the protégé needs to face.

The other type of careless mistake is the one that reveals a new insight. Think of Alexander Fleming's accidental discovery of penicillin. An accidental fungal contamination of his staphylococci cultures changed disease treatment forever. While it is unlikely your protégé will have such

Foster Accountability 107

a discovery, it can be worthwhile to ask the question, "Did you learn anything new or unexpected from the mistake?"

As a mentor, you want to remind your protégé that you are creating a safe place where you can plan to take risks (that may fail) as well as examine how the risks turned out (success or failure). When planning the risks, help your protégé strike a balance somewhere between baby steps and reckless abandon. When failure occurs, remind your protégé that failure is a natural part of learning. In the safe place of mentoring, you can help your protégé come to see that mistakes and failure are rarely as bad as we fear, and most mistakes contain something to learn from.

It may help open up the discussion of failure if you are able to tell your protégé about something you tried that failed. Use some of the questions below to get you thinking about your own mistakes and failures:

1. What small but important mistake have you made in the last six months?

2. What happened as a result of the mistake? How did you feel when you realized you made a mistake?

3. What did you learn from the mistake?

4. What was one of the more significant failures you have had in your career? When was it? What made it a failure?

5. How did the failure affect your journey? What were you feeling as you went through the failure?

108 *Foster Accountability*

6. What did the failure teach you? How did it change your thinking? How have you used the failure to teach others?

Celebrating Success

Much of this chapter has focused on helping the protégé through "the struggle" of learning. We have looked at barriers to action as well as the failure that often accompanies learning, focusing on your role as a mentor to guide your protégé through the growth process. Depending on what challenge the protégé is tackling, the struggle may see many ups and downs. Your role is critical to seeing your protégé through the downs. When your protégé comes through the struggle and seems to have made the learning permanent, you should pause to acknowledge the work he put in and the results he achieved. More than acknowledging success, you should celebrate it.

While every protégé's particular struggle is different, what they all have in common is the struggle itself. Barriers were overcome. Fears were faced. Comfort zones were traversed. Assumptions were challenged and rewritten. Perspectives were changed and new approaches were mastered. And, you were a witness to all of it. In fact, you may have been the only one who knew how difficult the struggle was. People around your protégé may have noticed something different, but they may not know what changed or how difficult the change was. So, you may be the only one who can appreciate how much the change means to your protégé.

Over the years, I have found that celebrating success is actually difficult for a great many mentors. For some, it feels awkward. For others, it doesn't occur to them at all. While there is no one formula for celebrating success, you can use the guidelines below to help you.

Keep it in character. If you are not an overly expressive person, it may feel awkward to both you and your protégé for you to jump up and down and scream, "You did it!" Find a way to express your excitement that is in keeping with your overall character. Also, be mindful that you and your protégé may prefer to celebrate in different ways. Take your lead in celebrating from what would be most meaningful to your protégé.

Make it proportional. Find a way to match the celebration to the level of struggle. Something that took a long time and effort for the protégé to overcome deserves something more than a pat on the back. And, something smaller doesn't need a parade. Think about a similar struggle you faced and what would have been the right amount of acknowledgement and celebration.

Celebrate progress. You may not want to wait until the protégé has completely mastered the challenge. There will likely be opportunities to

Foster Accountability   109

celebrate small wins along the way. These minor victories can be meaningful to keep progress going. They reinforce the protégé during the period of Conscious Competence to keep her from losing momentum.

Link effort to outcomes. When praising success, remember to praise both the actions the protégé took that were different and the results that were achieved. "I am so glad that you got the promotion that you wanted. I am especially proud that you had the courage to ask for it. I know that wasn't easy for you."

Keep it genuine. Before congratulating your protégé for success, make sure that your praise is genuine. Nothing can be worse than deflating your protégé's moment with praise that is forced or even tinged with disappointment. Think about the time when you had a small win of your own and someone important to you said, "I'm glad you made it this far. I do hope you can go further." Even if your protégé's success may be overcoming something that is not a challenge for you, remember that it is a challenge for her. Empathize as best you can and make the celebration a genuine reflection of your pride in her accomplishment.

Fostering accountability is where all of the work of mentoring often pays off. Anyone can give advice and tell someone what she ought to do. Staying with your protégé through the struggle in a safe and supportive way creates opportunities for tremendous growth. All of the investment that you and your protégé have made can pay off in ways neither of you could predict. Celebrate the success together to commemorate what you accomplished on the journey.

References

Adams, L. (2011). "Learning a new skill is easier said than done." Gordon Training International: www.gordontraining.com/free-workplace-articles/learning-a-new-skill-is-easier-said-than-done/.

Allen, D. (2015). *Getting Things Done: The Art of Stress-Free Productivity.* Penguin Books.

Duhigg, C. (2012). *The Power of Habit: Why We Do What We Do in Life and Business.* Random House.

Gollwitzer, P. M., and Sheeran, P. (2006). "Implementation intentions and goal achievement: A meta-analysis of effects and processes." *Advances in Experimental Social Psychology,* 38, 376–90.

Vygotsky, L. S. (1978). *Mind in Society: The Development of Higher Psychological Processes.* Harvard University Press.

Yeager, D. S., Purdie-Vaughns, V., Garcia, J., Apfel, N., Brzustoski, P., Master, A., Hessert, W. T., Williams, M. E., and Cohen, G. L. (2013). "Breaking the cycle of mistrust: Wise interventions to provide critical feedback across the racial divide." *Journal of Experimental Psychology: General,* 143, 804–24.

8 Fill the Toolkit

Cynthia's fingers drummed on her desk as she stared off into space. She glanced at her notes from her last few meetings with her protégé, Roman, and then resumed staring, hoping an answer would come to her. He's getting bored with our meetings, *she worried. Roman was a vice president of software engineering for a startup company that had about thirty employees, while Cynthia was a director of software architecture for a large company with over 20,000 employees. She had signed up to participate in a mentoring program focused on helping startup companies get to the next level. The first four months of their meetings went well, and she felt like she was learning as much from him as he was learning from her.*

But, two months ago, their meetings seemed to lose some energy. The topics he wanted to discuss were ones that she hadn't encountered before. "How do I build an engineering culture that will support our growth?" Roman asked during one meeting. "I'm not sure," Cynthia replied. "I haven't had to build a culture before." While she tried falling back on asking Roman questions to prompt his thinking, she was unsure of what questions to even ask. She felt like they were from different worlds. She had always worked inside of large organizations and took for granted a lot of the issues that Roman was having to build from scratch. On the other hand, she led an organization of sixty, which was twice the size of his entire company.

She saw an alert on her email program and stopped ruminating long enough to read it, happily welcoming the distraction. It was a note from a vendor asking if she was going to attend a two-day conference on "Transforming IT." Who has time for that? *was her first thought. She scanned down the list of speakers, stopping at a talk that caught her eye: Engineering Your Culture: From Startup to Growth. Her curiosity piqued, she performed a quick search for the speaker, which brought Cynthia to his blog, which had many posts about the importance of culture as startups pass through phases of maturity. One of the posts cited another author's* Harvard Business Review *article about revitalizing culture in mature organizations.*

Fill the Toolkit 111

Another alert startled her, reminding her of a meeting she had in fifteen minutes. She looked at the time and realized that she had spent the last forty-five minutes getting lost in all of the writing that had been done on a topic that she hadn't given much thought to before. She found the original email that had started her on this journey and forwarded it to Roman, asking if he could go to the conference with her. She quickly fired off another email, asking her assistant to clear her schedule so she could go. As she started pulling together what she needed to get to her next meeting, she paused to let a smile wash over her face. An hour ago, she wasn't sure what she was going to talk about with her protégé. Now, she thought the conference couldn't come soon enough.

Cynthia's experience is quite common. As mentoring relationships grow and mature, they often reach a plateau. The mentor and protégé are through the initial discovery stage that was fueled by the energy that comes from new relationships. They have explored some of the hands and head issues that brought the protégé to mentoring and find themselves running out of steam. New topics do not come as easily, or, as Cynthia and Roman experienced, the topics that do come are outside the mentor's area of expertise. In fact, it is often the fact that the early conversations come so easily that the partners don't know what to do when the conversation hits a lull.

The heart of the seventh rule of mentoring, Fill the Toolkit, is this: you don't have to have all of the answers. Part of what made Cynthia so comfortable with their early conversations was that they were inside of her comfort zone. The topics Roman brought up were ones where her experience and expertise were important inputs to the conversation. She could lend guidance to Roman, helping him think through the issues and come up with solutions. When they moved to other topics where she lacked expertise, she was somewhat embarrassed that she didn't have enough knowledge to give him her ideas or even ask insightful questions. She was stuck in the teacher part of the mentoring role and missed the fact that being a learning partner was just as important a role.

When you reach the point where you feel like you have shared everything you know with your protégé and your partnership is plateauing early, it is time to Fill the Toolkit. You are now in learning mode with your protégé, where your partnership will be an important force fueling the learning. Be honest with your protégé that you don't have the answers, but you will be willing to work with the protégé to find them. Admitting your own vulnerability can be difficult, but it will strengthen your relationship. Imagine being Roman receiving the email from Cynthia offering to go to the conference with him to learn about the topic that interested him. He is likely thinking that he hit the mentor jackpot.

Filling the Toolkit involves adding activities to the mentoring process to further the conversation. It can allow for both a broader conversation covering more areas as well as a deeper exploration of ideas meaningful

112 *Fill the Toolkit*

to the protégé. It builds on the prior rule, Foster Accountability, by creating accountability for homework and other activities between mentoring sessions. This chapter will familiarize you with a host of activities that you and your protégé can use as you continue to work together. Some I call **catalysts,** as they start you and your protégé on a conversation. Others I call **accelerants,** as they accelerate and deepen learning on topics. They can be used at the beginning of a partnership to get the two of you focused or when you reach a plateau point to recharge your conversations.

Catalysts

Sustaining momentum over the course of a mentoring partnership can be challenging, even with the most driven protégé. Building momentum often requires the help of catalysts to start progress or keep it going. What follows are different techniques that can spur mentoring along and create energy for a protégé to take action. The catalysts involve tools of self-discovery for a protégé that can be examined in the safe place of the mentoring partnership.

Personality Assessment

Each of us has a distinctive character that defines how we operate. Some of us are more extraverted, others more introverted. Some of us prefer structure and order to our worlds, others take the world as it comes and adapt. Personality is a complex set of tendencies and dispositions that influences how we see the world and interact with it.

Our personality is something that often goes unexamined. We don't often ask ourselves, "Why did I approach the situation one way while someone else approached it differently?" Personality is often at the heart of our individual strengths and weaknesses. For a protégé, an examination of his or her natural tendencies creates a great foundation for a mentoring dialogue. They form the foundation of many of our strengths and weaknesses; understanding them allows us to harness them better when they give us strength, as well as temper them when they are holding us back. Personality itself is neither good nor bad, so we don't examine personality looking for flaws. Rather, appreciating our natural differences helps us fit better into the world around us.

There are many options out there for analyzing personal tendencies, and not all of them are good. Nor are all of them available for the general public. Below, I will highlight three of the more common instruments that can be used.

DiSC. One of the more accessible measures is DiSC, which attempts to categorize personality into one of four dimensions: dominance, influence, steadiness, and conscientiousness. The basic report is rather simple to follow, but can give a protégé insights into how she or he comes across when dealing with others.

Fill the Toolkit 113

Strengths Finder. Donald Clifton created the Strengths Finder in 2001, and it is currently being marketed by the Gallup organization. The instrument provides feedback on an individual's "talents," or natural tendencies. There are thirty-four talents measured by the survey, and respondents get a report back on their top five talents. The test is relatively inexpensive, and the talents are fairly easy to understand and can be explored through the Gallup website.

Myers-Briggs Type Indicator. The MBTI is the strongest of the three mentioned. It is more complex than the other two, giving the respondent a richer view of her or his "psychological type." The report gives feedback along four dichotomies of personality: Extraversion-Introversion, Sensing-Intuiting, Thinking-Feeling, and Judging-Perceiving. The four dichotomies combine to form sixteen different psychological types. The "Step II" version of the instrument provides further detail into twenty sub-dimensions of personality (five for each of the four primary dichotomies). The MBTI usually requires a certified practitioner to administer and interpret.

There are many other options out there that can be used as well. At the end of the day, the personality measurement is intended to hold up the mirror to the protégé and give insight. Below are tips for working with one of the instruments:

1. No test will be 100% accurate. Instead of focusing on the part that does not feel right, focus on the part that does.
2. When reviewing the feedback, ask how the points in the report affect the protégé's real life. When do the tendencies work well? When do they get in the way?
3. Tie the observations and reflections back to the protégé's overall goals. How can the information be used to help the protégé get closer to her or his overall plan?

Career Values

Jacob was an IT manager at a manufacturing plant who was desperate for a new job. When he began working with his mentor, his primary focus was getting back the spark he had lost for his job. Over the prior two years, he was heavily involved in the rollout of a major new enterprise software package for his company. He was the liaison for his plant. He sat on the steering committee for corporate manufacturing, and had gone on two trips to the company's European headquarters during the project. But, now that the project was over, he was back to being the IT manager for his plant. He was an Explorer, and he wanted a change.

His mentor, Julia, was a senior director in corporate operations, and was well placed to help him explore possible career paths within the organization. Jacob said he was "open for anything," saying he could move back into a manufacturing role, move to the company's North

114 *Fill the Toolkit*

American headquarters in IT, or really anything. Before starting a wide-ranging exploration together, Julie suggested that he complete a career values exercise (see Appendix).

Career values are those attributes of a job which we value. Some of us want autonomy in our work. Others want to work with people we like. Still others want to do meaningful work. Each of us carries an implicit set of these values around, and we use them to evaluate how happy we are with what we are doing. Our values also change over time. The things a twenty-five-year-old wants from a job will be different from what the same person wants at forty-five.

A career values exercise makes these implicit values explicit, giving the mentor and protégé a chance to examine them in the light of day. Such an examination can give a mentor insight into what is driving the protégé's goals. It can also help refine and focus the goals, serving as a lens through which to evaluate opportunities.

Julia had Jacob look at the career values and sort them by importance to him. He selected his top eight values: Geography/Location, Stability, Work-Life Balance, Work with Others, Challenge, Significant Work, Status/Prestige, and Flexibility. When he finished, Julia said, "Now, we have something to work with. We can use these to help you find what you really want." She was startled with what he said next: "Actually, I think I already have it." They spent the next hour walking through the values one at a time. For each one, he explained how his current role met seven of the eight values. He said that the plant where he worked gave him a sense of security in his work, how it had a steady pace he found comfortable, and so on.

When he reached the final value, Challenging Work, he said, "This one is what has been driving me. That two-year project was so interesting and challenging. I guess when it ended, it left a big hole that I have been trying to fill." That revelation changed the tenor of the conversation with Julia. He realized that he really was a Homesteader: he had the job he really wanted, he just needed to change it to one that engaged him again. The focus of their mentoring changed from finding a different role to helping him find ways to take on more challenging work in his current one.

Not every protégé experiences the epiphany that Jacob did. But, many of them gain valuable insights into what is driving them by looking at their career values. Many are surprised by their final list, especially as they recognize how it may have changed over time without them realizing it. When using such a list with a protégé, keep in mind several things:

1. No job is going to be a 100% match for all of our values. Find a role that gets you most of the way there.
2. Not all of our values are equal. Some values are more important to us than others. When using the list of most important values, talk about which are the most valuable, and use those to guide the discussions.

Fill the Toolkit 115

3. The list of values can be influenced by what is going on right now in the protégé's world. Revisit it from time to time to see if the list has changed at all.

Once you have your list of values, it can be used to both examine the protégé's current role and explore possible future roles. For examining a current role, you can help the protégé identify elements of her job that aren't meeting her needs and find ways to change that. For examining future roles, you can engage in great discussions that help the protégé learn more about future possibilities and make thoughtful choices about next steps.

Personal SWOT Analysis

In the chapter Chart a Course, I described how you can use a personalized SWOT analysis to help your protégé analyze where he is today in relation to his envisioned future. In using this catalyst, you ask a protégé to take a somewhat comprehensive look at himself in relation to both his goals and the environment in which he is operating. The thought exercise is meant to help the protégé step back from the landscape and consider what about himself will enable or prevent his accomplishment of his goals (the Strengths and Weaknesses portions of the SWOT), and what in his environment will make it easier or harder to pursue his goals (the Opportunities and Threats part).

While I described it as a step in the process of setting mentoring goals, it can be used at any time during the mentoring process when a protégé has to assess his current state against his goals. It can be especially useful in tackling thorny head issues that are complex and start to feel over-whelming. It is also useful to help brainstorm new strategies that the pro-tégé hasn't tried when the current strategy doesn't seem to be working. After your protégé has completed the exercise, use the questions below to take the conversation forward:

- What is missing? (After you have worked with your protégé for a while, you should have a sense of where his strengths and weaknesses are. You can offer your own feedback to the SWOT if there seem to be omissions.)
- How can you better leverage your strengths? Are there other approaches you can take that would better capitalize on them?
- How are your weaknesses getting in the way of your strategy? How can you minimize their impact?
- Are you taking advantage of all of the opportunities you have before you? Sometimes an opportunity can be to involve others in solving the problem. Are you trying to do all of this yourself?

116   *Fill the Toolkit*

- Are the threats as big as you think they are? Are you cutting yourself off from a course of action because of your fear of a threat?
- Is there an opportunity hiding in the threats? Sometimes, a threat can be seen as an opportunity when viewed through a different lens.

Multi-Rater Feedback

For the protégé who makes the transition from individual contributor to manager, a whole new set of skills become important. In fact, we are often promoted to leadership roles because of our technical skills and not necessarily for the potential we show for leadership. More importantly, the protégé who is a leader is affecting others around him, and his effectiveness is more determined by how successful his subordinates are.

The most difficult part of mentoring a leader is the constrained view of reality that you have: you are limited to the protégé's view of the world, including all of his blind spots about leadership. As a result, any guidance or advice you give is based on the view of the situation through your protégé's eyes. One way to get another perspective is through a multi-rater feedback process, which is also called 360° feedback.

A multi-rater feedback process involves collecting the perspectives of the protégé's subordinates, peers, and boss. Most 360s are computer-based, and produce reports that summarize feedback from the different perspectives, usually rated against a leadership competency model. The advantage of such a process is that it provides somewhat anonymous feedback, which allows different parties to give feedback they might hesitate to do otherwise. Often subordinates (and sometimes peers and even bosses) avoid giving feedback directly for fear of the repercussions. A 360° feedback process creates a safer way to share feedback that is important for the leader to hear.

Processing through multi-rater feedback with a mentor can be a powerful way to identify developmental goals for a protégé. It is important to emphasize the role of the safe place within a mentoring partnership when processing feedback. Many leaders have a hard time reading the feedback reports, as they may be receiving feedback that they haven't heard before. It helps to have an ally like a mentor who can help process the emotions that can come with reading a feedback report. Another part of the mentor's role is to help ensure the protégé reads and processes what is being said. Many leaders find themselves arguing with or dismissing the feedback, saying things like, "They don't understand," or "That is not what I meant to do." Help your protégé get past these impulses, as they defeat the purpose of the feedback. Keep in mind the following phrase: "It doesn't matter what you think you are doing; it matters what they think they are getting."

Below are some basic tips for helping your protégé process the feedback:

1. Start with overall reaction. What are the impressions of the feedback in total? What confirmed what the protégé already knew? What was a surprise?
2. Look at overall highs and lows. Which areas got overall high and low marks? Talk about how those tendencies show up in day-to-day work.
3. Compare self-ratings to other groups. Most multi-rater feedback assessments ask the participant to rate him or herself. Look at where the protégé's self-ratings were higher or lower than other groups. Ask what those groups might be seeing differently.
4. Compare groups to each other. Being a leader requires us to wear many different hats and presenting different faces to different groups. Often you can start an interesting discussion by looking for differences between the groups in their perceptions of the protégé. For instance, you might find that the protégé gets very high ratings from subordinates on the same competency for which peers or the boss give low ratings. You might ask, "What do you think your peers (or boss) are seeing differently than your subordinates?"

At the end of the day, a multi-rater feedback report can feel overwhelming, especially with the volume of information that it can contain. Your best bet is to help the protégé focus on one or two areas that would give the biggest gain in the near term or best align with the protégé's long-term goals. Use these areas to focus action for the near term in the mentoring partnership. A lot can also be gained by revisiting the report in three months to either mine it for more information or to check in on progress, comparing what the protégé has been doing to what the original feedback was.

Accelerants

While the catalysts described above are meant to either jump-start a protégé or reenergize one, the accelerants are meant to keep momentum going and build it over the course of the mentoring partnership. They allow you to go deeper into topics of interest or deal with hurdles that are impeding progress. Treat the following tools like homework that will prompt more action and help move your protégé along.

Reading Assignments

If you are like me, you have a stack of books on interesting topics that you keep meaning to read, some of which you started and threw onto the stack after a chapter or two (I applaud you for making it this far

118 *Fill the Toolkit*

into my book). You may have a directory on your laptop or in your email program with links to articles that you will read when you have some time. You know that once you finish them, you are usually better for it. Sometimes you pick up tips that you can apply. Other times, the reading helps you think differently about a situation you are facing. But, the reward of these insights are often insufficient to overcome the other priorities that are keeping you from having the time to read.

Wouldn't it be great if someone created some accountability for you to tackle that stack of books? You can be that someone for your protégé. There are likely many articles and books written that address the hands, head, and heart issues your protégé is facing. As a mentor, you can help your protégé identify these sources and overcome the inertia that is keeping her from spending the time reading them. The steps to meaningful reading assignments are relatively simple.

First, find out what topics would be interesting. They can come directly from the goals for mentoring that you identified at the beginning of the partnership. The topics may also arise from the regular conversations you are having. Once you have potential topics in mind, you can start scanning your environment for sources that can help. There are numerous articles, blog posts, podcasts, and videos that speak to what your protégé wants to learn. Perusing the *Harvard Business Review* website (hbr.org) or the TED talks site (ted.com) can reveal brief interesting articles or speakers who can help open the door to a topic. Often, they can be a jumping-off place to other sources, such as longer articles or books. To get started, ask your protégé to look for sources that would be interesting. You may also spend a little time scanning these sources yourself to see what you can find. Look over your own bookshelf for readings that were insightful for you.

Once you have located a good source, make the assignment. As we discussed in the prior chapter, we are wired to not want to disappoint someone else. Ask your protégé to review the source and have it ready for your next meeting. Doing so will raise it on your protégé's priority list and increase the likelihood that she does it. For books, you probably want to break it up into manageable segments, like two to four chapters (depending on length) between meetings. You will want to set aside some time yourself to do your own homework for the last step.

The final step in fostering accountability for reading is setting aside time in your next meeting to discuss the reading. You might find that the reading was so engaging that the two of you can easily launch into the discussion. If not, you might use the questions below to get you started:

- What was your overall reaction to the reading?
- Which ideas were most interesting?
- What insights did you get from the reading?

Fill the Toolkit   119

- What was missing from the reading for you?
- What other questions or ideas do you have now?
- What did you take from the reading that you can put into action?

Of course, the reading is not an end in itself, but merely a starting place for dialogue. It is meant to spur discussion, further your protégé's learning, and lead to new actions that can be taken. Encourage your protégé to describe tangible actions that can be taken. And, see if this reading leads to other interesting sources that can be the topic of the next meeting.

Pro/Con Lists

Greg was a talented software engineer for a high-tech startup company. He joined the company when it just had twenty employees two years ago. Now, the company has 200 employees, and he is considered a veteran. Last week, his manager said that, with the recent growth, they were going to be promoting a few of the engineers to supervisor and she wanted to know if Greg wanted to be considered.

Greg went to meet with his mentor, Charan, to talk about it. Charan was another early employee who was now a director; Greg figured if anyone could talk to him about the decision to move into management, Charan could help. While Charan gave Greg some great insights into the role, he still wasn't sure what to do. The day before Greg's boss had asked for an answer, he and Charan met for two hours to talk about it. They went round and round the issues, ideas, and concerns, but didn't come to a resolution. The next morning, Greg's boss told him that, since she hadn't heard anything from Greg about the decision, that they had taken his name off the list. He was crestfallen, not because he had a burning desire to be a supervisor, but because the decision had been made by default because he couldn't reach a decision.

Many protégés find themselves stuck, held in place by some decision that they aren't facing directly. It could be the choice to accept a promotion, or the choice to let go of an employee. Your protégé may be struggling with staying in a job that isn't satisfying, or working for a boss who doesn't value his contributions. When we are in these situations, we have a lot of ideas swirling around our heads keeping us from moving forward. There are reasons to stay in the job (I have only been in the job for nine months; I don't want to look like a job hopper) that are fighting with the reasons to leave (the job isn't what they described during the interview). These internal conflicts often give way to inertia: continuing on the current path instead of making a change. If you have a protégé who is dealing with this internal conflict, a simple pro/con list can help shed light on the opposing forces and open up a discussion about what to do about them.

120　*Fill the Toolkit*

The idea itself is simple: draw a line down the middle of the page, and list the reasons for staying on one side and leaving on the other. While you can do this during a mentoring meeting, such a list is best done as homework so the protégé can set aside some time to reflect on it. When the list is complete, you can spend time going through each item on the list. Let your protégé lead the discussion, and ask questions to understand each item. The exploration may take some time, but it will help you to focus on the conversation your protégé needs to have.

Pro/con lists can many different forms:

- **Choice A/Choice B**: Greg's decision was to make two pro/con lists, comparing the pros and cons of staying an engineer with those of becoming a supervisor. It is natural that some of the cons for one list may also be pros for the other list.
- **Energize/Drain**: If you have a protégé who is struggling in her current role, ask her to keep track of how she spends her time over the next two weeks. Put the activities that give her energy on one side, and activities that drain her on the other. This list can help her figure out how she might need to recraft her job or focus her efforts in thinking about her next role by focusing on jobs that have more of the energizing column in them.
- **Excites/Scares**: When facing a potentially emotionally laden choice, it can help to get the emotions onto the page. Have your protégé list the things about the opportunity that excite him on one side and those that scare him on the other. Getting the emotions out of his head can help him make a more rational choice.
- **Benefit/Risk**: A different take on the same exercise is a benefit/risk analysis, which asks your protégé to weigh the choice more rationally. This version of the exercise works well for strictly head issues, but often leaves out the heart side of the equation. If the protégé still seems stuck after this rational reflection, try the excites/scares list to zero in on the emotional components.

There are several benefits to a good pro/con reflection. It gets the ideas out of your protégé's head and into written form. From there, you and your protégé can talk about each point in turn, what each point means and why it is important. Second, it is a tangible action toward a decision. While it is not the decision itself, it is a step forward to taking some action. It builds some momentum toward the next step (whatever that might be). Finally, it can help identify more complicated head or heart issues that are getting in the way. By shedding light on them, you and your protégé can explore them and discover a path forward.

Of course, if you do discover a head or a heart issue, you may need to slow down and not push for action right away. Slow down and ask questions. Realize that the issue that is holding your protégé up may carry some emotional valence, and pushing for action may derail trust. Use empathy to connect with the protégé and feel the emotion with him. Then, when he is ready to move forward, start building momentum again by encouraging the next step toward action.

Transition Letters

While a good pro/con list can often surface heart issues, it may not be able to defuse the emotional component. Marie was facing a very difficult choice to leave a role she had as a softball instructor. She had been teaching pitching to girls part time ever since she finished graduate school. As her full-time job began demanding more of her time, she found that the instruction was creating too many conflicts. While she still loved the time she got to spend teaching the girls, she realized it was time to give it up.

It was a gut-wrenching decision for her, one that she had been postponing for months. Then, her mentor recommended she write a goodbye letter. He said that she didn't need to send it, but she did need to write it. Marie addressed the letter to all of the girls and their parents, explaining her decision and why it was so hard. Writing the letter was difficult and emotional. But, when it was done, she realized that she could make the decision.

Transition letters ask a protégé to truly address feelings that she hasn't brought fully to the surface. She needs to fully feel them before she can do anything else. When you suggest a transition letter, ask your protégé to address it to the people whom she fears hurting. Remind her that she doesn't ever have to send the letter or even show it to you. But, after the letter is written, talk about what it felt like to write it and how she feels now. This simple but powerful tool can help a protégé face the emotions that are holding her in place and begin to move forward.

Other Accelerants

There are many ways to accelerate a protégé's progress. The three ideas above are just a starting place. Below are other options that can help a protégé make progress. As you and your protégé work together, check to see if these accelerants might help the protégé further his goals.

Education/training/certification. Many protégés discover through their personal SWOT analysis that they lack the formal education or certification to accomplish their goals, or at least to be competitive with others. Options in this space range from those that require a great deal of cost and commitment (for example, a master's degree) to those that can be accomplished with relative ease (for example, an online course or a brief training program). Help your protégé brainstorm and evaluate options to

122 *Fill the Toolkit*

see which would be reasonable to undertake relative to her goals (especially those requiring more time or cost).

Conferences. While training programs can help a protégé close a specific skill gap, participating in conferences can serve broader purposes for a protégé. Consider Roman and Cynthia attending the conference on Transforming IT. They may have chosen to go to learn more about the specific topic Cynthia saw in the announcement. But, they have the opportunity to achieve a lot more. Roman can get connected into a larger community of other IT leaders in companies similar to his own, creating other opportunities for his development. He will also be exposed to thought leaders in his field who can connect him to other perspectives and expertise. By attending the conference together, he and Cynthia can spend a meeting or two dissecting what they learned from it, using it as a springboard for further discussions.

I realize that some seasoned professionals don't attend conferences, saying that they don't hear anything they didn't already know. I have sat in conference presentations myself and had the same thought. I heard a speaker at a conference (ironically enough) change my perspective. He said, don't go into a conference expecting to gain volumes of new knowledge. Instead, go on a treasure hunt for gold nuggets. Listen for small ideas that get you thinking. Write them down and think about them later. That nugget he gave me has changed how I approach conferences and has helped me use them as platforms to stimulate my thinking and give me new ideas to shape what I already know.

Public speaking. A slightly more challenging, but potentially more impactful, way to accelerate a protégé's development is to give talks on an area of the protégé's expertise. It is a way to increase the protégé's visibility while establishing herself as an expert. Preparing to give a talk also helps deepen expertise, as she may have to do extra research as well as be prepared enough to answer questions. A speaking engagement does not have to be as daunting as speaking at a conference. When the mentor and protégé work for the same company, many mentors will invite their protégé to give a talk to the mentor's staff on the protégé's area of the company.

As an accelerant, observing your protégé speak gives you a lot of directions to take a conversation. You can ask questions about the protégé's learning while preparing for and giving the talk:

- What did you learn while preparing for the talk?
- What did the group's questions tell you about how your group is viewed in another part of the company?
- What surprised you about the discussion that resulted from your talk?

You can also give your protégé feedback on her public speaking. Observe things like pacing, poise, visuals (if she uses slides or other visual aids), or how she handled questions. Make sure you schedule a mentoring discussion for shortly after the presentation so your feedback is fresh.

Challenging assignments. Protégés can accelerate learning by seeking special projects or other challenging assignments through the normal course of their work. There is a wide variety of special projects which your protégé could ask to work on, from improving processes to serving on cross-functional teams to accepting a short-term assignment in another function or geography. Unless you are the protégé's manager, you are likely *not* in a position to give these kinds of assignments to your protégé. But, you can encourage him to talk to his boss about them. Use his goals for mentoring as a way to identify what sort of challenge would be good and brainstorm options he might pursue. He can then ask his boss to open up such opportunities.

Informational interviews. Another good assignment for both Explorers and many Scouts is to conduct informational interviews with people in your network. As your protégé identifies areas she would like to explore further, you can connect her with others who can enlighten her. For instance, if your protégé wants to explore another department in your organization, you can connect her with someone you know in that department and have her set up a meeting and conduct a thirty-minute interview. While you might be able to tell her what you know, making the referral is more powerful for several reasons. First, the person she interviews is living in that department now and can share with her things that you may not know. Second, your protégé is keeping ownership of her learning by conducting the interview herself. She will undoubtably uncover new questions she wants to ask during the interview and take it in new directions. Finally, she will now have a new network connection that knows her. If an opportunity comes up later, the person she interviewed now knows her and can make her aware of it on the basis of their discussion.

Job shadowing. An extended and less structured version of the informational interview is job shadowing. A protégé can learn a great deal by spending time observing how someone else operates. Shadowing could involve tours of a location, attending meetings, or being introduced to an entire work group. It can be as short as a few hours and as long as a few days. In fact, several informational interviews could be scheduled during a day-long job shadowing experience. You may even consider "reverse" job shadowing by visiting your protégé's work and observing her in action. Such a visit will give you a lot of context for understanding her situation and the people with whom she is interacting.

These catalysts and accelerants are not tools unique to mentoring, nor are they comprehensive of everything that your protégé can do to accelerate learning. Tools like these are used regularly to develop employees all of the time. But, mentors often don't think of them as adjuncts to their mentoring process; instead they think mentoring is limited to the

124   *Fill the Toolkit*

mentoring conversations. Like Cynthia at the beginning of the chapter, the tools you can add to your mentoring toolkit are all around you if you know to look for them.

Reflection Journal

If you truly want to deepen and extend your protégé's learning, encourage her to keep a reflection journal on the mentoring experience. Some protégés may do this naturally, but you may want to encourage yours to do so. This journal is not homework you are going to ask your protégé to share with you. Rather, it is a chance to reflect on what you discuss and draw new insights or reach new conclusions. Taking time to think about a learning experience helps the lessons learned and the skills acquired become more fully integrated into the protégé's thinking. In fact, Shantz and Latham (2012) demonstrated that participants in a learning program learned significantly more if they took time to write down their reflections after the experience than those who did not.

Keeping a protégé's reflection journal does not have to be complicated. It can be as simple as recording discussion notes and action items during a meeting, and taking ten minutes to review them and look for new insights after the meeting. If your protégé keeps a journal, you can ask her to review it every three to six months and have her bring in her thoughts about her growth. The reflection discussion can help a protégé realize how much she has grown over time and create an opportunity to celebrate success together.

(Re)Charting a Course

The mentoring tools covered in this chapter are just that: tools to facilitate a mentoring partnership. The real work of mentoring is helping your protégé learn and grow in ways that are meaningful for this time in his journey. It is important to not lose sight of this larger journey and, from time to time, to step back and take stock of where you are. The final tool for your toolkit is to review your protégé's mentoring goals and chart the next part of your journey together.

To start the process, ask your protégé to look over the original goals that she set at the beginning of the process when you charted a course together. If your protégé didn't set firm goals but rather selected topics of discussion, ask her to review them. For the goals or selected topics, ask your protégé what she has learned during the time since they were set. The learning might come from your conversations directly. It also might stem from application of the ideas you have discussed. If your protégé is keeping a reflection journal, she should read her entries dating back to when the goals were set or the last time they were reviewed. After she has reviewed her progress, then ask what goals or topics should be next. Have her think about the next six months to three years of her journey and chart a course that would help her keep the progress going. There are four typical approaches to recharting mentoring goals:

- **Revise**: She sets a goal in the same topic, but takes it to another level. She sets a goal that stretches her further and gets her outside of her newly expanded comfort zone to keep growing.
- **Rebuild**: She rewrites an original goal based on what she learned. Perhaps the original goal was, in retrospect, too ambitious. Or, the goal focused on the right general area, but on the wrong tactic.
- **Redirect**: She sets a new goal entirely. It may be the goal she set with you at the outset has been met. Or, it is no longer germane to what is important right now. She can set aside that goal for a time to focus on what will be more relevant.
- **Reaffirm**: She keeps her original goal and wants to keep working on it. The goal is still relevant and is providing direction to your mentoring conversations.

I would recommend an exercise like this every six or nine months, depending on the type of mentoring partnership you have. For formal programs that have a fixed end date, you should have this conversation every six months. If your partnership is less formal, with less frequent meetings and no end date, every nine months to two years is a good pattern. The exercise will keep your protégé focused on her journey and keep the energy up for your meetings.

It may also be that a natural outcome of this process could be a winding down of the mentoring partnership. The goals your protégé had for mentoring have been met, and she doesn't have another goal that she wants to pursue. In the next chapter, I discuss what to do when active mentoring is over and your time on the protégé's journey comes to an end.

Reference

Shantz, A., and Latham, G. P. (2012). "Transfer of training: Written self-guidance to increase self-efficacy and interviewing performance of job seekers." *Human Resource Management*, 51, 733–46.

Appendix: Career Values Exercise

A career values exercise is a great catalyst exercise that can open a protégé up to what is usually an unexamined question: How well does my work fulfill me? The conversation you can have from this discussion can go in many directions, and help the protégé see things he hadn't before.

126 *Fill the Toolkit*

Its power comes from its ability to take something very abstract (happiness and satisfaction with a job in the context of career values) and make it concrete. When it moves from conceptual to practical (e.g., What about your job makes you say you are not satisfied with the level of teamwork it gives you?), you can have a discussion of something that would otherwise be difficult to articulate.

Taking your protégé through the exercise involves three basic steps:

Step 1: Review the list of career values below. Circle or make a note of values that are important to you at this stage in your life/career. That is, when they are met they give you happiness, or when they are not met they make you frustrated:

Advancement opportunity	Knowledge/Research
Adventure/Risk-taking	Leading others
Affiliation	Make decisions
Altruism	Meaningful work
Autonomy/Independence	New technology
Career growth/Progress	Opportunities to learn
Challenge	Personal growth
Change and variety	Physical challenge
Competition	Power/Authority
Creativity expression	Professional development
Excitement	Recognition for work
Fast pace of work	Stability
Financial reward	Status/Prestige
Flexibility	Teamwork
Friendships	Use technical skills
Fun	Variety
Geography/Location	Work alone
Help others	Work with others
Influence others	Work/life balance
Interesting work	

Step 2: From the list of all of the values, select **up to eight** that are your top values. These are the values that bring you the most happiness when met or cause the most frustration when not met. List the Top 8 values in the table below. Describe why each value is in the Top 8. What about it makes it important to you?

Step 3: Rate your present level of satisfaction with each of the Top 8 from 1 (very dissatisfied) to 5 (very satisfied). Try not to let your mood today or this week sway your ratings. Think about how satisfied you have been over the last three to six months. Then, describe what about your current situation caused you to rate that value that way.

Fill the Toolkit 127

Values	Why in Top 8?	How satisfied? (1–5)	Why satisfied (or not)?
Value 1			
Value 2			
Value 3			
Value 4			
Value 5			
Value 6			
Value 7			
Value 8			

Questions to explore the values: Use the questions below to delve into the meaning behind the values.

1. How does your satisfaction with your values affect you at work?
2. How do the values balance each other in terms of your overall satisfaction? That is, what tradeoffs are you making where you are accepting lower satisfaction of some values for higher satisfaction with others?
3. How has your satisfaction changed over the last few months? What contributed to that change?
4. How has your list of Top 8 values changed over the last three to five years? What changed for you that shifted your values?
5. As you consider possible future roles, how well do you think they will help you satisfy your values?

9 Honor the Journey

Henry put down his phone as he was suddenly transported back to graduation day five years ago. Marius stood before him beaming with pride with the light tan hood draped around his neck. Not many of the MBA students come to commencement, but Marius said he wouldn't miss it. Henry spent a lot of his time mentoring students, but none compared to Marius, who brought an intense curiosity to their discussions, which were wide-ranging and intellectually stimulating. Marius consumed entire books on topics he wanted to discuss with Henry, and elevated their discussions of strategy, finance, and operations to a philosophical level. Henry sometimes felt like he was learning more from their discussions than Marius, but almost every discussion ended with, "Thank you, professor. You have really helped me understand this topic better. I don't know if I could make it through this program without your help." More than any other protégé, Marius pushed Henry to be a better mentor.

All of that made graduation day bittersweet for Henry. He was so proud of Marius, but he also knew that their partnership was coming to an end. Marius grabbed Henry and hugged him, thanking him over and over again. Marius said that he wanted to keep their meetings going, and that he would get on Henry's calendar in a few weeks. After a few months of silence, Henry reached out to Marius to see if he wanted to get together and reminisce. His message went unanswered for a few more weeks when he got the reply, "Would love to! I'll reach out when I'm back in town. Major plant expansion. Can't wait to catch up with you." That was the last Henry heard from Marius. Until today.

From the call, Henry learned that Marius found himself in a bind and really needed his old mentor's advice. He was in the middle of a career dilemma. On the one hand, he had an offer for what would have been his dream job five years ago. On the other, he had a counteroffer from his current employer that would match the salary of the other job and give him an ownership stake in the company. The dream job would require him to relocate his family and spend about 50% of his time on the road. Five years ago, that would not have been a problem. Now, his kids were older and he was hesitant to be absent for so much of their middle school years. Marius said he had gotten advice from his friends, but he really trusted Henry and wanted to know his thoughts. He apologized for not reaching out for the last five years, but he hoped Henry could meet and help him think through his situation.

Henry is an experienced mentor who has worked with hundreds of students in his career. But, few other protégés have illustrated the last rule of mentoring more clearly than Marius. We are all on our own journeys of exploration throughout our careers and our lives. We are constantly confronted with challenges that require us to change our thinking and to learn along the way. Just like in Homer's epic *Odyssey*, there are times when a mentor enters our lives and travels part of the journey with us. As time goes on, however, circumstances change, and the time of that mentor comes to an end. It is a natural part of every mentoring partnership, one that should be celebrated more than mourned. The protégé's journey will always be bigger than the part any one mentor plays in it. At graduation, Henry struggled in letting Marius go. He knew that their enriching meetings would come to an end. Despite Marius' reassurances, he knew that things were changing and that they wouldn't have their conversations when time passed so quickly, with three hours feeling like thirty minutes. In those weeks and months after graduation, Henry comforted himself by reflecting on the role he got to play in Marius's journey, knowing that he made a difference.

As difficult as it was to let their relationship become dormant, Henry did so in a way that created the opportunity for the call that he just received. He realized that one of the best jobs you can have is that of *mentor emeritus*, an honored position that one earns in recognition of good service. Despite the fact that Marius allowed the partnership to grow quiet over five years, he still viewed Henry as an important guide in his life, and wanted to reach out to rekindle their mentoring, even if it was just to help him think through the current situation he was facing. All of the trust and empathy that passed between them during the period of active mentoring still held currency for them and is what caused Marius to reach for the phone when he did.

As your protégé progresses down her journey, the need for and nature of mentoring will change. The change can be abrupt (for example, Marius graduating and becoming immersed in a new job) or subtle and experienced over time, with meetings becoming more infrequent or sporadic. The change can have many causes (which we will explore below), and it usually brings about a redefinition of your relationship. Some mentors fear the end when they sense it approaching. They believe that if a protégé begins to pull away that it is a reflection on the quality of their mentoring, or more personally on them as a mentor. However,

130   *Honor the Journey*

the change rarely has anything to do with the mentor. It is generally a change in the protégé's journey that has brought about the change. When you sense that you are approaching a transition point with your protégé, you should embrace it instead of running from it. The final rule is Honor the Journey, with the emphasis on the fact that it is the protégé's journey.

The cause of the change can take many forms. In some cases, it is a simple change in the protégé's work situation. You may work in the same department, on the same floor, or on the same projects. The proximity made it easy for you to work together where neither of you had to expend much effort to get together, and serendipity put you in the same place at the same time. Or, you were both enrolled in a mentoring program, which created the structure for your meetings. When the mentoring program comes to a close, the common project ends, or your protégé takes a role in a different location that eliminates the opportunity or impetus to meet, you may find more and more time passes between meetings. More dramatically, your protégé may leave the company where you both work or graduates from the school where you teach, as Marius did. When you become "out of sight, out of mind" to each other, it can be natural to let a relationship that had been very active fade. It is not a reflection on the strength of the relationship any more than it is on the fact that you had not established any routines about getting together that were more involved than dropping by and seeing if your protégé was available for lunch.

Other mentoring relationships wind down as the protégé's focus changes. The protégé's initial reasons for seeking a mentor either lose immediacy or relevance to the protégé, or the goal of mentoring was met. In either case, the drive that was there at the beginning fades, and the protégé doesn't pursue the relationship as strongly. Again, these reasons have less to do with the quality of the relationship than they do with the protégé's situation. Instead, take comfort in the fact that you were able to meet the protégé's need for one stage of her journey.

It is not uncommon to feel a sense of loss when the partnership ends, especially if it fades more quickly than you thought it would. Henry knew that Marius would eventually graduate and move on, just as many protégés did before. Knowing that the transition was coming didn't make it any easier. It is, however, a natural part of any developmental partnership: eventually the junior partner grows, learns, and moves on to the next challenge. Mentoring shares this quality with parenting (though usually to a lesser extent).

Transitioning the Partnership

Most mentoring partnerships end without any acknowledgement that they have ended. Even partnerships in many facilitated mentoring programs end only with an email from the program coordinator

Honor the Journey 131

letting the mentors and protégé know that the program has concluded. When you see a transition in your partnership coming, consider the following steps:

1. **Lead by Following**. The first rule of mentoring still holds true even at the end. Follow the protégé's lead as the partnership winds down. You can invite the protégé to meet to reflect on the time you spent together, but let him decide whether to have the meeting. Suggest a location that will allow you to celebrate the time you spent together and the successes your protégé has had. If your protégé is not open to the idea or unresponsive to your contact, send a final note thanking him for the time you had to work together. Share your reflections and learning from the partnership (see the next step) and leave the door open (the third step).
2. **Reflect Back**. If you are able to get together for your final meeting, use it as an opportunity to reflect on your time together. Talk about what you both learned through the process. In the last chapter, I encouraged you to suggest for your protégé to keep a reflection journal. You may want to do the same. Almost every mentor with whom I have worked learned something from every protégé. Share what you have learned from your protégé and what you learned about being a mentor. If your protégé expresses gratitude for the time you spent with him, accept it graciously. If he asks you how he can repay you for your help, say, "You can't repay me, but you can mentor someone else. Look for the opportunity to do for someone else what I did for you."
3. **Leave the Door Open**. Like Henry at the beginning of the chapter, give the protégé permission to reach out to you in the future. Some will take you up on it right away. In fact, what was meant to be a wrap-up meeting can reenergize a partnership that was fading. Your protégé may want to keep in contact with some regularity for a time. However, most protégés will be more like Marius. You may not hear from him again for years, or ever. One of my personal regrets was not keeping in touch with Dr. McMillan from Chapter 1 (something I hope to rectify by the time the second edition of this book is published).

When You Need to End It

To this point, I have described partnerships that ended after a period of time that was marked by productivity and positivity. The vast majority of partnerships I have seen have been of this type. There are some circumstances, however, when the partnership needs to be actively ended by the mentor. These situations may involve some difficult feedback for you to deliver. But, it is better to address the issue than to let it fade while

132   *Honor the Journey*

harboring negative thoughts or feelings about the partnership. Consider ending the partnership in the following cases:

- **Lack of time.** Sometimes one or both of you cannot make time to meet together with any regularity (especially in a facilitated mentoring program where you have a fixed period of time). You may have overestimated the time you would have to be a mentor. It is better to let your protégé know that you will not have the time rather than put her through the exercise of looking for availability on your calendar that truly does not exist.
- **Failing to lead.** Some protégés view mentoring as a passive experience and expect the mentor to do all of the work. He expects you to set the meeting schedule and bring all of the topics for you to discuss. If you have communicated that you want him to take the lead and he still doesn't, you would be better off devoting your mentoring time to someone who will.
- **Upward delegation.** Related to failing to lead is the protégé who asks you to do all of the work between meetings. If you find yourself doing more work between meetings than your protégé, you may have someone who is delegating to you. Remind yourself that this is the protégé's journey, and sometimes he has to go through the struggle to learn. Don't let him delegate the hard work of learning to you.
- **Breaking confidentiality.** The safe place of mentoring can lead both of you to taking risks and sharing information, ideas, and feelings that are truly private. Breaking that trust can bring a relationship to a quick end. It is commonly the mentor who has to be mindful of confidentiality. But, there are times when you are the one showing some vulnerability. If your protégé is the one who breaks the confidence of the partnership, do not hesitate to bring it up.
- **Political behavior.** In one of the first facilitated mentoring programs with which I worked, we had a protégé who was having difficulties with her boss. The two of them had strong disagreements about the direction of her work. When she brought up her side with her mentor, she failed to present her boss's side or share that there was a disagreement between the two of them. Instead, she got her mentor's feedback, and then used her mentor's position within the organization to contradict her boss. Since she had access to someone in the organization who held a higher rank than her boss, she was using her mentor as leverage. This sort of political behavior is not only damaging to the mentoring partnership, it threatens any culture of mentoring that may exist within an organization.
- **Personal problems.** When you open the door on a helping relationship, you may find that there is a lot more going on than you anticipated. What looks like a struggle with focus or self-confidence may yield much deeper issues with which the protégé is grappling. There

Honor the Journey 133

may be problems with a marriage, children, an aging parent, or other psychological or financial conditions that are beneath the surface. You may be unwittingly wandering into a situation you are not equipped to handle. While it is important not to make your protégé feel abandoned if he wants to bring up these issues, you are better off encouraging him to get help from a professional. Consider saying, "I feel like the issues we are discussing are well beyond my expertise or ability to help. Can I help you connect with a professional who is in a better position to help you?"

When you find yourself in one of these situations, share your feedback with your protégé. Discuss the challenge you see in the partnership and see if there has been a misunderstanding. If you feel the partnership can continue, you may need to spend time rebuilding the trust that has been lost. You will need to recreate the safe place for both of you, which may take some time.

If after sharing your feedback you still believe the relationship cannot be repaired, you may need to withdraw entirely. Thank the protégé for the time the two of you were able to spend together and express regret that mentoring was not able to work out. If the problem was scheduling and lack of time, you may want to leave the door open for when you and your protégé may be able to make mentoring a higher priority. If the issue was a conflict about roles (not leading or upward delegating), you can leave open the possibility of reengaging on different terms in the future. If it was a situation of broken trust, you may need time apart for the emotions stirred up by the infraction to dissipate. Even if you aren't going to leave open the possibility of a future relationship with this protégé, you should try to learn from the experience. What did you learn about yourself, your protégé, and about mentoring? What did you learn about communicating and negotiating expectations? What did you learn that you can apply to your experience with your next protégé?

No Two Protégés Are the Same

And, I hope there is a next protégé no matter what brought about the end to a mentoring partnership. My wish is for you to continue to share your gifts with others who are looking for guidance from an experienced mentor. Mentors I have worked with over the years continue to teach me that no two protégés are the same. Each mentoring partnership takes on its own dynamic based on the two individuals involved and the journey they are both traveling. Each will have different needs and different learning styles. What came easily with one protégé may be a struggle with the next one. One protégé may need an accountability partner, while another needs a thought partner. One needs a safe place to vent, and the next needs the hard look in the mirror that comes with feedback.

134 *Honor the Journey*

The real secret to mentoring is that you never stop learning. Every mentoring experience you have, either as mentor or protégé, will teach you something if you are open to it and look for it. Look for opportunities to share your gifts with others, and they will share their gifts with you. True success comes not from what you achieve, but what you help others to achieve. True wealth comes not from accumulating, but from sharing.

Now that you are at the end of this book, put it in a place where you will find it easily for your next protégé. Use it to refresh yourself on the rules for mentoring since you may have a different focus that emphasizes a different set of mentoring rules. I regularly have to review the mentoring rules with every new protégé to remind myself not to push too much advice or take the lead. You will learn something new each time you read the book as you will deepen your understanding of your own skills as a mentor. And, when you tell your protégé to mentor someone else, give her or him a copy of the book to get started.

Thank Your Mentors

Before you go, I have one more request of you: thank your mentors. You have not achieved what you have and reached the position you occupy without the help of countless others. Some may have given you brief inspiration, while others may have given you years of counseling and guidance. Some created opportunities for you and others gave you the courage to act. Go back to that list from Chapter 1 where you wrote down the names of ten mentors. When was the last time you were in contact with them? Do they know what impact they had on you?

Resolve to thank each of them. You can send emails or handwritten notes. You can invite them to lunch or dinner, coffee or cocktails. Tell them what you learned from them and how they helped you. Tell them how you shared what you learned from them with others. Show how their investment in you has multiplied and is handing down wisdom. Let them know that what they did had meaning for you. It is the meaning they created that will continue to give meaning to the time they spent with you.

Index

accelerants of progress in mentoring 8, 24, 112, 117–24
accountability 13, 40, 76; beginning with a question 100; fostering of 98–100, 104, 109, 112, 118; of mentor *and* protégé 99
action steps 100
advice-giving: by the mentor 13, 30, 65, 134; proper place for 67, 77–8
advocacy role of the mentor 5
affect 59
Allen, David 102
altruism 6
Amabile, Teresa 59
ambition in the protégé 35
aspirations of the protégé 9–10, 35
assumptions made by the protégé, challenging of 54–5

baking analogy 10–11
barriers to action 101–3
"belief barrier" 75
beliefs, letting go of 92
"benefit/risk" listings 120
boss–subordinate relationship 8–10, 17, 99, 132
Burch, Noel 97

career development 30, 34
career exploration: both *size* and *type* 41–3; options considered in 37; phases of 37–42
career values 113–15; exercise on 125–7
careless mistakes 106–8
catalysts for change 98, 112–13
celebration 108–9
certification of education or training 121
challenge questions 71–2

challenge projects 123
change: desire for 76–7, 90; fear of 91–2; strong forces in opposition to 92; *see also* catalysts for change
changing course 49
charting a course 12, 43–6, 124–5
chasing a protégé 28–9
Clifton, Donald 113
coaching 5, 33
"comfort zones" 53, 98, 104–5
communication media 25
competence, *conscious* and *unconscious* 97, 103–4, 106, 109
complicated tasks 102
conferences, participation in 122
confidant role 4–5
confidentiality 60–1, 132; limits to 60
confirmation bias 82
"connector" role of the mentor 5, 7–8
control, sense of 35
conversations as part of mentoring 43–8; focus for 46; jump-starting of 46–7; recharging of 111–12
"counselor" role 5
crooked paths followed in the course of a career 22–3, 41
current work interfered with by mentoring 9

days chosen for recurrent meetings 26
decision-making 119–20
"defender" role of the mentor 5–6
defensiveness on the part of protégés 31–2
delegation of work from protégé to mentor 132
dependence on the mentor 66
disappointing a mentor, fear of 100–1, 118
disorderly progression 41–2

136 Index

distance mentoring 25–8
Duhigg, Charles 103
duration of mentoring meetings 24
dynamic nature of mentoring
  relationships 10

Edison, Thomas A. 104
emotion–feedback cycle 81–2
emotion words, list of 83–4
emotional load 67–8
emotional release 52–3
emotionally-laden choices 120–1
emotions 81–8, 94–5; *multiple* or
  conflicting 84
empathy 13, 80–4, 92–4, 102, 121;
  as distinct from sympathy 81; steps
  towards 82–4
employee development 123
empowerment of the protégé 20–1, 24
ending of a mentoring relationship
  125, 129–34; brought about by the
  mentor 131–2
energy: derived from new learning
  105; needed to sustain a mentoring
  partnership 34–5, 94–5
"excites/scares" listings 120
experimental mistakes 105
exploratory questions 70–1
Explorer type 37–8, 42–5, 123
eye contact 27

facilitated mentoring 7–8, 12, 17,
  24, 130–2
failure: fear of 105; as a natural part
  of learning 107
fear: of disappointing a mentor 100–1,
  118; of letting go of beliefs 92; of
  making mistakes 105; of upsetting
  the current situation 91; of what
  needs to be done to reach goals 102
feedback 28, 48, 74, 81–2, 133; from
  mentor to protégé and *vice versa*
  61; on public speaking 122–3; *see
  also* multi-rater feedback; "wise
  feedback"
"Feel, Felt, Found" technique 87–8
"feeling questions" 84–8
feelings: addressing of 121; naming of
  83; validation of 81
Feld, Eugene 3, 98
"felt need" in the protégé 19–20
final meeting between mentor and
  protégé 131
fitness goals 99

Fleming, Alexander 106
frequency of mentoring meetings
  23–4, 58
frustration, expressing of 52–3
future need for an established
  relationship 55, 133
future-oriented focus of mentoring
  33–6, 43, 47

getting to know one another (mentor
  and protégé) 22–4, 56–7, 66; useful
  questions for 57–8
goals of mentors 19–20, 60
goals of protégés 30, 33–9, 43–9, 88,
  113–14, 124; for Explorers 46; for
  Homesteaders 46; for Navigators
  46; for Scouts 46
grievances, airing of 52

habits: difficult to change 103;
  returning to 106
"hands" issues 68–9
Harris, Sydney J. 76
Harvard Business Review website 118
"head" issues 68–79, 82, 103, 115, 120
"heart" issues 68–9, 81–2, 89, 94,
  103, 120–1
Homer 129
Homesteader type 40–3, 46
"homework" 94–5, 112, 120; for the
  mentor 118
hope, giving of 93
Horowitz, Ben 19

incompetence, *conscious* and
  unconscious 97, 103
inertia 88–93, 118–19; sources of
  91–3, 103
informational interviews 123
insight questions 70–4
"inspirer" role 4
interpersonal factors 55–6, 59
interruptions to mentoring meetings 59
"invested" in mentoring 17–18
issues discussed with mentors,
  anatomy of 67–9

job shadowing 123–4
judging your protégé 93, 100–2

Kram, Kathy 52

language differences 27
Latham, G.P. 124

Index 137

leadership by protégé, failure of 132
leading by following 12, 16, 20–2, 28–30, 39, 46, 66, 69, 93, 131
leading by the mentor, consequences of 18–20
leading questions 30
learning: definition of 97; four-step model of 97; from mistakes and failure 53, 104–8; as a hard-fought process 104
learning journals for recording mentoring experience 60
learning partners 111
Levi-Strauss, Claude 63
life cycle of a mentoring relationship 13
listening skills 27
location of mentoring meetings 24–5, 59

McMillan, Marvin 1–3, 25, 131
managers as mentors 8–10; *see also* boss–subordinate relationship
managers of protégés, contacts with 60–1
masters degrees 121
meals, meeting over 22, 57, 59
mentor emeritus position 129
mentor roles 4–6, 16–17, 116
mentoring: concern with learning 97, 134; definition of 2–4, 7, 16; *formal* or *informal* 7, 125; limited view of 123–4; phases of 7; rules for 10–11, 134
mentors' own mentors 18
mistakes: fear of (but learning from) 104–8; "good" and "bad" 105–6
momentum: building of 121; sustaining of 112, 117
motivation of protégés 4, 19, 100–1
multi-rater feedback 116–17
Myers–Briggs Type Indicator (MBTI) 113

naming of feelings 83
Navigator type 39–46
networking 13, 38, 123
note-taking 27, 60

open-ended questions 30
opportunities, analysis of 44–6
optimism 35
"ownership" of problems and solutions 66, 123

painful circumstances preferred to the fear of change 91
partnership with the protégé 6, 20, 22, 102, 177; differences between individual cases of 133; maintenance of 28; *see also* learning partners
Pasteur, Louis 41
patience, need for 62
penicillin, discovery of 106
personal interests 23
personal problems 132–3
personality assessment 112–13
"plateaus" in mentoring relationships 111
"political" behavior by the protégé 132
potential seen in the protégé 17, 20
power differences between mentor and protégé 17, 21–2, 25, 66, 99
praise, genuineness of 10
"present" when meeting 59
priority for mentoring meetings 58
problem-solving 18–19, 29, 66–7, 73
pro/con lists 119–21; different forms of 120
progress, celebration of 108–9
"progress principle" 59
psychological types 113
psychosocial support 52
public speaking 122–3

questions: advice-laden 30; *exploratory* type 70–1; *insight* type 70–4; mentors' use of 13, 30, 69–78; power of 64–9; sent in advance 36–7, 44; *see also* "feeling questions"

readiness, testing for 86–7
reading assignments 117–19
reflecting on the past 6, 36
reflection journals: kept by mentors 131; kept by protégés 124
relationship between mentor and protégé *see* partnership with the protégé
respect for the mentor 22
retrospective view of mentoring 6, 36
risk-taking 53–4, 93, 107
risk transfer 17
role models 4
running 10–11

"safe place" creation 9, 12–13, 28, 33, 35, 47–9, 51–4, 72, 89, 93, 97, 100, 104, 107, 116, 133
SARA acronym 73

138 *Index*

scheduling of time 21, 24–8, 58–9
Scout type 38–46, 123
Shantz, A. 124
shared experience 81
silence, filling of 29–30
similarity between mentor and protégé 55
skills as a mentor 59–60, 134
small wins 59, 109
Socrates 66
"sounding board" role 5, 71
"sparks" that ignite mentoring relationships 7–8
spontaneous mentoring 7–8, 12
status quo as a powerful force 92–3
stepping back 87–9, 124
"Strength Finder" 113
stretch mistakes 105–6
struggling for solutions 19, 93–4, 104, 108–9, 132; mentors getting drawn into 48
success: celebration of 108–9; desire for 18, 100
support: for faltering mentoring relationships 8; for the protégé from the mentor 103–4
SWOT analysis 44–5, 115–16, 121
sympathy 81
symptoms, working on 65, 89–90

"taking over" as a mentor 29–30
taking stock 124
TED talks website 118
telephone conversations 25–7
thanking your mentors 134
threats, analysis of 44–5
360⁰ feedback 116
time, lack of (as a reason for failure of mentoring) 132
time available for mentoring 21, 24, 58

time frames for looking ahead 37
time scheduling *see* scheduling of time
time spent on different activities, monitoring of 120
time zones 27
times of day chosen for recurrent meetings 26
"toolkits" 13
training programs 121–2
transition letters 121
transition points 130
transitioning a mentoring partnership 130–4
trust 4–8, 12–13, 22, 51–62, 132–3; definition of 51; as the foundation of mentoring 52–62
"trust accounts" 56
trust propensity 55–6, 62
trustworthy actions 56

understanding the protégé's situation 80–1
"ups and downs" in mentoring 108

video calls 27
virtual tours 27
vulnerability: on the part of the mentor 111, 132; on the part of the protégé 51, 62

"why", avoidance of 72
winding down a mentoring relationship 125, 130–1
"wise feedback" 106

Yeager, David 106

Zone of Proximal Development (ZPD) 104

PGMO 07/12/2018